THE Long White Glove

DAVID CHORLTON

THE Long White Glove

Uncovering the truth
behind a murder mystery
from Vienna.

All rights reserved. Published by New Meridian, part of the non-profit organization New Meridian Arts, 2023.

LIBRARY OF CONGRESS CATALOGING-IN-PUBLICATION DATA

The Long White Glove
Authored by David Chorlton

ISBN: 9798985965988
LCCN: 2023935801

Thanks to Ernst Ebm for the photographs.
Photograph of Ernst Ebm on page 88 is by David Chorlton.

The story:

My personal recollections
will be obvious from the following
text, while other details are drawn
from the many newspaper and magazine
articles once in the possession of
Gerhard Eder's father, Walter. He had
also kept many official typewritten
documents from Gerhard's treatment
after being arrested. I did meet
Ernst Ebm in 1993, and he told the
story he had uncovered in his work
as a reporter, including the name of
the man to whom the evidence Ebm and
two colleagues had discovered led.
I have initialized names of officers
involved in interrogation, as Herr
Ebm had initialized Ingenieur Josef
R.'s name in his articles closer to
the time the events took place. It
has been primarily my intention to
tell what I learned about Gerhard
Eder's experience.

For information on those
mentioned throughout the book, see
the Appendix at the end.

one

From the park, I cross Prinz-Eugen-Straße and go to Schwindgasse, which is as empty tonight as it must have been when the man I am following walked quickly along this sidewalk between the characteristically heavy architecture of apartment buildings with dirt balled in his fists and the taste of a woman's skin in his mouth. Listening for his uneven footsteps, I stop at the point where he dropped a handkerchief not far from house number 3, with its plaque indicating that it was once the home of Hugo Wolf. A few steps farther along is where a black glove had fallen to the ground. Next is Argentinierstraße, a longer street. He turned right here, then left onto Gußhausstraße. Is anyone following me? I stop to look back. Still quiet. By the time I reach Karlsgasse, my pulse has quickened. Right, then left to Frankenberggasse, yet another short street among many whose intersecting shadows contribute to the mystery of a well-worn city. It ends at Wiedner Hauptstraße, which is busy during working hours but on this Saturday evening, carries little traffic. Reassured that nobody is watching me, I cross with a hand inside my coat, as if to grip a bundle of clothes, the discovery of which would testify to my guilt in one of the most shocking events to happen in Vienna since the war ended.

Noting that a purse was dropped where I am standing, I decide I must hurry all the way to Waaggasse. A few steps and I reach Schäffergasse. A nylon stocking slips from my imagination and slithers onto the ground just before I turn right onto Preßgasse. Now I see something familiar to me, the market area of the Naschmarkt. This is deserted ground on a Saturday evening, with only a prostitute watching for customers between the empty wooden crates, stacked and waiting for Monday. "No," I tell her, "I'm not interested," and I head for the public toilets. They are open tonight, as they were those thirty-six years ago when a man stopped to wash his hands and happened to drop a golden earring on the ground next to the sink like the period at the end of a teasing sentence, unwittingly leaving the final clue before he disappeared. There is little to interest me now beyond recent graffiti demanding that foreigners leave Austria. Outside the toilet, I know I have escaped, but there is nothing in the map, nothing I know about this murder that tells me where to go from here.

two

A Sunday in November of 1971 was the day after my arrival in Vienna to stay rather than just to visit family during a hot August flavored with my favorite cold raspberry soda. My uncle, Norbert Eder, had just taken me out on the first of many day excursions we took together into the countryside around Vienna. This one had been, as was usual in the winter months, taken beneath a grey sky that pressed down on us and muffled our conversations outdoors as we visited the village of Gumpoldskirchen and the monastery at Heiligenkreuz, stopping en route for a meal.

Returning to the city late afternoon in fading light, Norbert steered his sporty little car through the third district, which I knew was not on the direct route to his apartment. As we reached Prinz-Eugen-Straße, Norbert drove slowly and continued to do so as we passed Schwarzenbergpark. Without taking his eyes from the road before him, he calmly took his right hand from the steering wheel and pointed toward the park. "That is where Ilona Faber was murdered," he said with no further explanation of who this Ilona had been. The surprise silenced me.

Neither of us spoke again until we had reached Norbert's home on Ruckergasse in the Meidling district. After parking, he led the way to his ground floor apartment and had me sit down while he made us some tea. His lighting was minimal, the furnishing elegant if spare. The presence of several potted plants softened the atmosphere. The place was tidy and impressive for a man who lived alone after his second divorce. On the walls was a number of the photographs Norbert had taken and which were very important to him. Just before he went into the kitchen, he stopped, bent down, and pulled a trunk from under a table. He opened it, revealing a stack of newspapers, magazines, and other official-looking documents. He rummaged inside it, and when he found what he was looking for, he pulled it out and held a long white glove in the air before me between his thumb and index finger. "This is the glove," he said, "Ilona Faber was wearing the night she died."

three

On the evening of April 14th, 1958, at the end of the showing of an Elvis Presley film at the Schwarzenberg cinema, Ilona Faber was snatched from the street and forced into the park across the street by a man who subsequently rendered her unconscious before stripping her naked while Police Officer P. stood close by in the rain. Any officer stationed in Schwarzenbergplatz knew he was there to watch over the hated Russian monument in case someone set off a diplomatic crisis by attacking it. When he was questioned the following day, Officer P. said, "I stood in front of the obelisk as I was ordered to. In front of the obelisk were fresh wreaths and flowers, and I would have been in trouble for sure had even one ribbon been torn away or a wreath damaged because I had gone off to another area of the park."

Ilona's mother had tried to dissuade her from going to the cinema. "That is no film for you," she said as Ilona prepared to go out. Had Ilona's father been home instead of on a business trip, he might have succeeded where Frau Faber failed. Ilona, a typist by day, had been attending modeling classes. That is where she ought to have gone on this Monday night, but she insisted that she'd already covered the material for tonight's class. She was a blonde twenty-one-year-old sufficiently aware of her attractiveness to say, "Hardly has someone looked at me for the second time, when he already tries to kiss me." There was no suitor waiting to meet her. Elvis was the man she went out to see.

Five minutes would have been all the time needed for her walk home. She would not have crossed the street to go through the park because that would have taken her in the wrong direction. As ill luck had it, Ilona realized as she was about to leave the cinema that her pink umbrella was still lying under her seat, so she went back to retrieve it. By the time she finally went outside, the other patrons had already hurried away to get back to their dry homes. Perhaps the perpetrator had been inside the cinema and intended to follow her. Perhaps he had been waiting outside and seized his opportunity. Either way, he was strong enough to take Ilona and do whatever he wanted to before burying her in the wet soil using his hands as shovels. Had she been able to scream, surely the police officer would have heard. Ilona's mouth was stuffed full of soil to keep her quiet, and choking caused her death, as the medical examiner ascertained. He was also able to confirm that whatever pleasures the assailant took, intercourse was not among them, although teeth marks on the girl's breasts and pubic area indicated some of what he had enjoyed.

four

Discovery of the body occurred on the morning of April 15th as Officer Rudolf B. walked routinely along the path near the Schwarzenberg trees. Looking for nothing in particular, he caught sight of a white patch against the dark soil and bent down to pick up what he assumed to be a piece of paper. It was in fact an item of ladies' underwear. Suddenly alerted to the possibly something was wrong, Rudolph B. looked around and found first a pink umbrella, then a pale oval which turned out to be Ilona's face.

After being sealed off, the park quickly became the focus of curiosity for crowds gathering to get closer to the shiver of fear the murder sent through the city. The immediate investigation revealed that the assailant had taken as many souvenirs as he could carry, including underwear, a heart-shaped keyring, black nylon purse, lipstick, wristwatch, and a pair of golden earrings.

Some items had been dropped, indicating the escape route, which went as far as the public toilet on the Naschmarkt. An earring was found later in the day by Julius Liebewein, a jeweler who had no idea he had found evidence in a murder case until he handed it over to the police after taking it home to weigh in order to ascertain its value. That was insignificant except to show that Ilona's assailant stopped off, one assumes to clean himself up, before going home. The last item to be discovered was lying on Wehrgasse, which meets the Naschmarkt near the Kettenbrückengasse rail station, not far from the web of streets along the escape route. Only a few minutes' walking time from where the earring was dropped, lay a long white leather glove.

"Go to the nearest police station, place the earring on the table, and say 'It was me.'" So wrote Reinald Hübl in the Neuer Kurier, appealing to the murderer to step up and confess. "Add it up. How old are you? Add seventeen years in prison."

Not everyone was happy to accept seventeen years as the maximum in Austria for a crime. Talk of the death penalty was introduced in the political sphere. In vain, despite the priority given to a study of public safety in the Parliament now that sex-related murders had come to lodge firmly in the local consciousness. Among recent victims of unresolved crimes were Anna Eder, whose body had been dismembered, and pieces of which were discovered in the River Wien and the Prater; Elli Kastner, who was stabbed in the "Kalten Gang" case; and Maria Glock, attacked during a bicycle ride and stabbed to death. Hübl saw this latest murder as an escalation of the violence: "But with Ilona Faber, we carry something else to the grave. We are burying the belief in the safety of our city. We are almost tempted to bury our belief in humanity. Are we in such a position today that a young girl is in danger when she walks in the streets alone?"

five

Every five minutes, one potential witness or other reported having seen a neighbor coming home unusually late, a suspicious character boarding a tram or some other such observation.

Nonetheless, an arrest needed to be made, and one was. Given the constant watch afforded Schwarzenbergpark, anyone who spent much time there became conspicuous. One man in particular stood out. Johann Gassner had frequently been observed by officers and even greeted them with a cordial wave. He showed up on most nights and was tolerated as another fellow living on the sexual fringe and bothering nobody who didn't share his interest. Unemployed, thirty years old, unobtrusive in appearance with neatly combed black hair, Gassner came from Drosendorf, a small town to the north close to the Czech border. He was the eldest of the six children who survived the eight born to their parents. He had been a difficult boy, with troubled school reports describing him as prone to lying, egotistical, and lazy. Since coming to Vienna, he had become linked with homosexuals, lived off proceeds from prostitution, and spent short periods in jail for minor offences. He was, in short, as a character plucked straight from the fringe of society, the ideal suspect.

Gassner's photograph appeared on the front pages of the dailies on April 24th after six days of secrecy following his arrest. The carriers of news were unhindered by any need to think of a suspect as being innocent before he had been given due process, and next to a picture of Gassner was a bold black arrow and the bold face declaration: THIS IS HIM. There had been evidence to implicate Gassner with Ilona's murder, specifically a shoe print that matched his found in the park near where the body had been found. Explaining where he had been during the night spanning April 14th and 15th, Gassner described his nocturnal wanderings after waiting for someone who failed to appear, and he had headed off toward the Naschmarkt. On Schönbrunnerstraße, not far from Wehrgasse, he had breakfasted at a street kiosk on a bowl of gulyas. Close examination of Gassner's fingernails, however, showed no sign of any dirt residue, and therefore the authorities had no material evidence to merit detaining him any longer.

Hardly had Gassner been returned to the streets when he was arrested a second time when another shoe print matching his was discovered near the Naschmarkt public toilet. This time, he was in possession of a cigarette case in which he had a sketch of the area and a note to the effect of his having seen the murderer at a specific time after midnight. More determined this time, the investigators took their prisoner to the Court Medical Institute, where Doctors Schwarzacher and Breitenecker examined him. The most intense attention was directed toward Gassner's teeth and the marks left on Ilona's body. A dental expert, Doctor Zinner, was brought into the proceedings. To make things worse for Gassner, a lady companion said he had come to her urgently in need of a clean shirt and that he was a very driven personality. Trial was set for June 15th of 1959.

six

Hopeful citizens formed a long line along Alserstraße. Gassner entered the courtroom in a loose-fitting prison uniform that made him look like a clown. He faced a battery of flashes from eager photographers. Dr. Walter Macher, his attorney, appealed for the picture-taking to stop. Gassner did not deny the minor charges of embezzlement and petty theft, but when asked how he wanted to plead to the murder of Ilona Faber, he firmly claimed he was not guilty.

Prosecuting attorney Dr. Otto Hörmann placed Gassner in the basement of Viennese life, in the company of prostitutes, and portrayed him as a stereotypical killer with a record of trouble going all the way back to childhood. "Did you like going to school?" he asked. Gassner's embarrassed reply was that he sometimes used to play truant. An account of his adult life only added to the image of a potential murderer. Back in 1956, he had lived with a forty-year-old woman, Franziska K., on Wiedner Hauptstraße. When she died of a sleeping pill overdose, examination of the body showed she had been abused after death, although no charges against Gassner were made.

As the trial proceeded, mistakes in the protocol surfaced. Facts had not been entirely checked out. The head of the murder commission, Dr. Heger, had relied too heavily on the word of officials whose sloppiness became apparent as witnesses noted discrepancies between Gassner's explanation of events now and earlier when first questioned. Careless work, however, was not enough to slow the prosecution. After stressing the matching pattern of Gassner's shoe with the print near the spot where the earring was discovered, Dr. Hörmann anticipated clinching the case with testimony from the dental expert. The question on which Gassner's future hung was addressed to Dr. Hermann Zinner. The clock showed nine forty-five in the morning when Dr. Zinner was asked whether, after studying Gassner's teeth, he could reach the compelling conclusion that the bite wounds on Ilona Faber's body could only have been made by this man. Dr. Zinner replied firmly, "No, I cannot do that."

Dr. Zinner followed up by explaining that the wounds were made by a set of teeth notably similar to those of the accused. A second dental expert, Dr. Petri, testified that the kind of abnormality present in Gassner's teeth were by no means unusual and that of 206 people of Gassner's age he had studied, 8.2 per cent shared a similar feature. Medical examiner Dr. Boltz told the court that sexual intercourse was not carried out in the course of the crime against Ilona Faber, so there was nothing to be gained by ascertaining Gassner's blood group.

The prosecutor attempted to make up lost ground with a rambling closing statement, which embraced the calculation that Gassner had worked only 360 days during his thirty years of life. Dr. Macher, in his closing defensive argument, spoke concisely to dismantle the case against Gassner, ending his hour-long speech with an admonition to the jury, "Do not believe that you will release the public from its fear if you convict Johann Gassner. You cannot say a man is guilty only in order to produce a murderer."

After seven days in court, the eight members of the jury listened for three hours to legal instruction before retiring at one-thirty in the afternoon. Less than four hours later, the light went on to signal that a verdict had been reached. Four jurists voted guilty of murder, four voted not guilty. Johann Gassner was found guilty on the lesser charges and sentenced to three years in prison with the intent to have him moved later to a work house. Given the opportunity to appeal the verdict, he said, "High Court, I am thankful for the acquittal on the murder charge, but I would like to appeal the high punishment and being sent to a work house."

seven

Stepping from the train and onto the plat-
form at Westbahnhof in August just a few weeks
after Johann Gassner's acquittal, I was an eleven-
year-old thrilled to be back among members of
the family lucky enough to live in a city so much
more fascinating than industrial Manchester. My
diminutive grandmother waited to meet us in the
company of my Auntie Hele, her son Bernhard,
and my Uncle Norbert. We went together to the
one-room-plus-kitchen that comprised Maria
Eder's apartment on Lacknergasse in the district
of Währing. While the adults launched into their
discussion at a rate too fast for me to keep up
with, I stepped onto the little stool Maria Eder
had placed by the window so she could raise her
own tiny frame high enough for her to look out of
the window and down onto the street where the
tram made the final loop on its route, or across
the rooftops to the towers of the nearby church.

Leaning out just a few inches enabled me to look along a street where around midnight, a horse-drawn wagon used to bring milk into Vienna, stopping at the dairy shop in the next building on the street, where the milk was always refreshingly cold early in the morning, when I loved to run down the stairs to buy breakfast items.

The room itself was a monument to loneliness. Maria Eder lived alone, having been long separated from the husband, Dominik Eder, who had drifted off into a cloud of alcohol, leaving her with four children. The fifth, my mother, never found out, at least officially, who her father was. She often claimed she'd been told the man's identity was in one of my grandmother's diary volumes collected in small orange notebooks she bought at the shop up the street and around the corner, a shop stocked with paper of all textures and run by a lady who wore a dull grey smock and was dedicated to all the details of her trade. "We'll find out one day," my mother used to say, but when one day arrived, she obeyed the old lady's request and delivered the diaries to the flames. Here was one family scandal finally guaranteed of secrecy.

Although the usual population of the room was one, it contained beds enough for three or four in anticipation of visiting relatives from England or France. Two iron-framed beds, of the sort one might find in a hospital, were placed side by side with their ends against the wall that featured the print of a sentimental picture of Mary Magdalene rolling her eyes in crepuscular biblical light and an industrially produced weaving that showed a stag in brown and orange. The third bed stood lengthwise at the foot of the other two. This arrangement left little space for walking about.

A heavy-duty wardrobe contained the coats that made winter tolerable, plus extra pullovers. A chest of drawers contained the clothes she rarely wore. These were gifts which, along with towels and bed sheets, she would never need and which she kept faithfully wrapped to honor their function as presents. In glass cabinets were all remaining gifts, which collectively kept a geographic record of where her daughters lived and where her sons had traveled to: Mauberge in France, Paris, Venice, London, or Manchester. Here were the teaspoons embellished with city crests, a glass globe filled with water and imitation snow, ash trays purchased for their decorative value and given to one who never smoked. In the kitchen, the insides of the cupboard doors were a gallery of clippings from the colored weekly magazines widely distributed in Austria. The British royal family faced us whenever we went to fetch a glass to drink from or a plate. Collecting these pictures taken at Balmoral or Buckingham Palace was Maria Eder's tribute to her English son-in-law, her favorite.

Every time one of us needed to go to the toilet, we had to take the medieval-sized key that hung on a hook by the door and go out to the landing and that smallest of rooms shared with two other apartments. For collecting water, we went to the common faucet near the top of the stairs with the white enameled bucket kept for the purpose. The relative inconvenience of toilet sharing and water carrying were no impairment to our pleasures and the rush of happiness we felt on the occasion of a family transcending distance and coming physically together. While Hele and my mother, Erna, chewed into open sandwiches and recent family history, I played with my cousin, Bernhard, and when the games grew boring, we laughed half in English, half in German over scatology.

eight

In 1959, Gerhard Eder was fifteen years old. He had combed his hair back and greased it in the fashion of the time, which made him look much more than four years older than I was. His father wasn't with him at this small family gathering in Hele and Leonhard's apartment, but Norbert and his wife Inge were.

Gerhard seemed happy to meet his aunt who had left for England, if slightly embarrassed at the attention he received. Hele was an enthusiastic agent in bringing everyone together, especially in drawing her shy nephew into company. The one remaining feature that stood out with Gerhard was a tattoo on his arm. Somewhat clumsily, the name BRIGITTE ran along his arm. I thought of Brigitte Bardot, the best-known Brigitte of the day, but the name in fact referred to our cousin Gitta in France. Gerhard had spent time with her when she last visited from Mauberge with our

Auntie Elsa and her husband Andre, and he had taken a strong liking to her. At home in Neusiedl, where we subsequently went to see Gerhard again days later with the rest of Walter's family, he looked less at ease. He ran errands, went to restock cigarettes and wine while Walter Eder played host.

The final scene of our visit was, as ever, the parting at the railway station amid weeping and an air of *Who knows when we'll be together again?* as a voice struggled through the loudspeaker, announcing the departure of the Ostend Express. It may as well as have said, *Erna and Fred are leaving now with their son to be parted from those who love them.*

nine

Like Ilona Faber three years before her, Brigitte Besztenlerer died in a park after leaving a cinema alone. On Ash Wednesday, February 15th of 1961, the feature at Maria Enzersdorf, a small town to the south of Vienna, was a film about the jungle that provided a welcome if brief escape from the cold, foggy weather outside. The thirteen-year-old girl should have followed the main street all the way home, as that would have been the direct route with little possibility of her getting lost even in the fog. All she needed to do was to follow the street until she passed the Scheidpark and reached the family house just beyond it. She should have been home a quarter of an hour after leaving the cinema.

Margarete Besztenlerer looked at her kitchen clock at seven forty-five. This left her enough time to reach the cinema before the film was due to end, at eight o'clock. Mothers worry, especially when the weather is so bad. At eight o'clock, she stood outside an empty cinema. "There, I was told the film had ended much earlier. I wondered why I had not met Gitti on the way. I quickly went back to the house." Even in the thick fog, it was just possible to see across the street, so she knew she had not passed Gitti walking in the opposite direction. "My daughter was not at home. Then, an unspeakable fear came over me for the child. I fetched my husband, and together we set off to look."

"Gitti, Gitti, where are you?" Frau Besztenlerer called, as she remained alert to any movement in the fog. When a voice did respond, it was that of Gitti's grandmother, who happened to be wearing a headscarf just like the one the girl had on when she left home. The old lady suggested the girl must have stopped at the church on her way. Not surprisingly, considering the time, the doors of the church were locked. Margarete went to the local Gendarmerie office to report her daughter missing.

"Get along with you," the officer on duty said to her. "Who would be so afraid? Just because the girl is half-an-hour late in getting home, we aren't going to issue a missing person alert. She has probably met a friend somewhere."

The officer was not inclined to leave his warm room to go outside as long as he felt there was no basis for panic. On her way back toward home, Frau Besztenlerer found a group of people that included her husband, Gitti's grandmother, and an acquaintance, assembled near the Scheidpark. The acquaintance claimed to have heard noises coming from the park. "Maybe Gitti was in there playing games. You know girls will do silly things at her age."

Sparking the flame on his cigarette lighter, Michael Besztenlerer walked into the park. Having once lived in a former barrack there, he knew it well and found nothing unusual until he was about to turn back.

A piece of clothing lay on the ground beside the stone foundation to the former villa which once occupied the site. Herr Besztenlerer bent to look closer. A twig snapped. He thought someone must have been scrambling through the trees. It was almost nine o'clock. Gitti's body lay half naked with her pullover pushed above her breast, where blood trickled from a knife wound to the heart. The father took hold of his daughter's wrist to feel for a pulse. Nothing. Reigniting the cigarette lighter, he walked on and then spun around to rush back to the street. "Have you seen Gitti?" Margarete asked. "Yes, she…" And the expression on the father's face completed the sentence.

ten

The first Gendarmerie officer joined the group within minutes to lead the way with his flashlight. He discovered first a shoe, then Gitti's coat, her handbag, and her underpants. More items: a sock, a glove, and the second shoe. Squad cars arrived. Spotlights were set up to illuminate the area around the body where the search for clues continued. An object reflected light from the ground. "Does this cigarette lighter belong to you?" the officer asked Michael Besztenlerer. "No."

Photographers joined the searchers to record each detail. Next to join in was a tracker dog. Its handler led it to Gitti's body, from which point it tugged on the leash and moved energetically along the downtrodden path leading to the fence running alongside Helferstorferstraße, parallel to the main street on the other side of the park.

The dog forced its handler to follow it through a gap in the fence, across the pavement, and onto the road. It veered to its right, continued for several meters and halted, whimpering, at the tramlines close to the stop for route number 360. Handler and dog returned to the body to repeat the exercise with exactly the same result. Medical examiner Dr. Norbert Wölkart arrived just before midnight. Taking stock of the situation, he concluded that when he left the park, the murderer must have been covered with blood.

On the following day, witnesses offered various observations relating to the Fog Murder. Alfred Knotek, a boy of fourteen who knew Gitti, said he met her outside the cinema and watched as she set off for home. "Close behind her, a man about forty or forty-five years old and about 175 to 180 centimeters tall was walking. He wore a leather coat. The man limped on his left leg. He had a dark hat on and wore wide trousers with the belt of his leather coat hanging loose. I think I have seen the man before. As he slipped along behind Gitti, he went out of my sight and into the fog." Such was the ensuing obsession with leather coats for which passengers riding the number 48 tram in Vienna were summarily taken for questioning because of their clothing. Three hundred men were alerted for the criminal investigation.

Josef Kalab was a tram conductor on route 360 and worked on the tram that passed Scheidpark shortly after eight-thirty on Ash Wednesday. He said he noticed an unusual occurrence at eight thirty-four when a man jumped onto his tram as it slowed near the stop. The man wore a brown leather coat open at the chest and a white shirt buttoned at the neck without a tie. He had a slim figure, low brow, and strong hands. The point at which he jumped aboard was exactly that at which the tracker dog had stopped twice. "He got off in Brunn or Perchtoldsdorf. It is possible that he took off his hat while he was on the vehicle. I can't say for sure anymore. But I do remember clearly the protruding chin and the strange expression of the man."

Another witness, a motorist, stated that he stopped when he saw a figure materialize in the glare of his headlights on Helferstorferstraße, also about eight-thirty, and added that the man had just clambered through a hole in the fence to the park. "I saw the man directly in the glare of my headlights and even had to brake when he ran out into the road." The man who slipped through the fence limped and wore a leather coat.

Meanwhile, the examination of Gitti's body revealed that her assailant was a secretor, which is to say his blood group could be ascertained from other bodily fluids such as sweat, spittle, or sperm, and that he was of the blood group A2.

A team of investigators was assembled under the leadership of Major S., including Inspectors R., Z., B., Fe., and Fo. They questioned several men, all of whom were subsequently released. Those who had attended the showing in the cinema were called to take the places they had occupied in the hopes of one empty seat remaining. That, so the investigators speculated, would have been the one occupied by the murderer, and they hoped that whoever was in the neighboring seats could identify him, but the attempt came to nothing.

eleven

On February 25th, an alarm went out from the Felsenkeller in Perchtoldsdorf, a picturesque town also along the route of number 360, when a man answering the description of the figure in the leather coat was seen. A day later, another conductor on route 360 noticed a limping man in a leather coat in his vehicle, traveling toward Mödling. One hundred and fifty reports in all were registered from people who believed they had information on the unidentified man.

Several possible suspects were interrogated. A car dealer based in Perchtoldsdorf, Hans Luksch, received a tip from a woman who thought she knew the murderer's identity. The Gendarmes followed up after Luksch reported this lead to them. They traced the man in question and spoke with him on March 11th, announcing afterwards with confidence that "He has an alibi."

Two weeks after the murder, Alfred Knotek followed up his observation from the foggy night by telling his father, "A few days ago, I saw the man in the leather coat again. You know, the one who was following Gitti. The one who limps, that everyone is looking for now. I saw him right near the Gendarmerie station, and he saw me too. Then, he immediately pulled his hat down over his face, turned around, and disappeared. I didn't dare go after him or fetch the Gendarmes. Well, Father, I was playing truant from school that day." And yet again, shortly after that, Knotek saw the same man clambering over the railway tracks at the station in Maria Enzersdorf.

The next clue came by way of a handwritten postcard, mailed at the end of February, to the investigative team: "Look for me! Sender: perpetrator."

One feature at a time, a phantom portrait was pieced together from the descriptions given by Knotek and Kalab. The face showed a square jaw, a low brow, and an obsessive stare. When the picture was published in the press on March 15th, a motorist from Vienna came forward to tell that someone had flagged down his car in Perchtoldsdorf hoping to get a ride into the city on Ash Wednesday. "I am absolutely convinced: that was my passenger. He got out at Matzleinsdorferplatz."

The publication of this speculative picture created a new tragedy. For all his forty-eight years, Franz Wolfram had lived in Maria Enzersdorf. His neighbors had been taking special note of anyone who wore a leather coat or limped, as Wolfram did. Wolfram's limp had been caused by an accident in which he broke an ankle. After this, he left his job as a butcher for one with the local firm of König and Bauer, whose premises were close to his home. As he listened to a radio news report about the man seen on the night of the Fog Murder, Wolfram realized that he fitted the description. "Anni, how can the broadcasters say something like that? The description fits me." His wife, Anna, knew that Franz had spent Ash Wednesday evening at home with her, and when she looked at the phantom portrait on the newspaper for March 16th, she didn't harbor any untoward thoughts but tried to comfort her husband by saying that thousands of men look like this. A work colleague looking at the same picture was straightforward in his response as he faced Franz Wolfram and said, "Look, it seems to me that you're the Gitti murderer!"

On the morning of March 17th, Franz had not come home after a night shift. His son began to search for him and went into an out-of-the-way shed near the workplace. There was Franz, hanging from a rope. In his coat pocket was a note reading, "Dear Anni, forgive me, but everybody looks at me and believes it was me who killed that poor girl. I swear to you, it was not me. I could never do such a thing. Live well, and greet the children and grandchildren."

Wolfram was buried next to Gitti Besztenlerer in the Maria Enzersdorf cemetery. In the gravedigger's opinion, Gitti's murderer deserved a double punishment.

twelve

Hans Luksch stopped to look up a client's number in the directory at a telephone booth in Perchtoldsdorf shortly after mid-March. The book opened to a page where the names began with the letters Rei… and on which blood was smeared, causing several pages to stick together. Luksch recalled that tram conductor Kalab mentioned whose passenger may have gotten off in Perchtoldsdorf on Ash Wednesday, and Kalab did not believe in coincidences. Perhaps, he thought, the perpetrator stopped here to wipe his hands on the absorbent paper or needed to make a phone call and was bleeding from scratches inflicted by his victim. Luksch needed to know whether the blood here matched the blood group, A2, of the murderer and went straight to the nearest Gendarmerie station to report his finding with the request that the stained pages be removed from the directory to be tested.

However, he was met with the traditional caution of an Austrian official.

"Ah, that doesn't work."

"Why?"

"I have to make a request here first to the Postal Executive to be allowed to tear pages from the telephone book. Otherwise, it would comprise an impairment of public property."

After briefly weighing the interests of telephone customers against those of justice, Luksch decided to risk incurring the wrath of the Postal Executive and invited an officer to accompany him to witness his act of vandalism. Once he had the pages in hand, the automobile dealer made his way to nearby Mödling. He took them to a doctor there, who agreed that the paper appeared to be bloodied. A second doctor dismissed the idea and said the stains came from red wine.

Directed to the Medical Institute in Vienna's Sensengasse, Luksch continued his odyssey when he met with Dr. Herbich, who was not particularly interested in the matter but agreed nonetheless to a test. A week later, Luksch went back for the results. An official at the institute denied knowing anything about blood and a telephone directory at first but later acknowledged receiving a page. "Pardon," said Dr. Herbich, "there was just a single page. More exactly, it was only part of a page. But on no account were there more. And moreover, there was just one, not very strong, bloody stain on it."

Luksch knew there had been several pages stuck together. Dr. Herbich rummaged in the files and triumphantly retrieved a paper from which he read the conclusion that the blood stains had come from an animal and were probably made by a shopper fresh from the butcher placing a package of meat on the directory.

Being thorough, Luksch had kept a small square from the pages in question. He asked the doctor whether a small square had been cut from the page he tested. No. Determined to overcome the incompetence of Austrian bureaucracy, Luksch took his small sample to another hospital for a second test. The result: blood group A2.

The blood stains in a
phone book in Perchtoldsdorf

thirteen

Tensions were high when my father parked the car outside the apartment block where Leonhard, a German national living in Vienna, had moved in with and married Hele while he dreamed about and worked on a small family house at the edge of the city.

Our first impression was of a handsome man who was strong and proved it with his handshake. We sat at the table for coffee and cake to background music from a recording of Freddy Quinn, whose sentimental songs about seafaring adventures were favorites of Hele and Leonhard. Leonhard looked across the table, his blond hair curving back in a wave from his forehead, while my father drank his coffee. Leonhard asked my mother to translate.

"Ask Fred what he thinks of Hitler."

My mother did just that, and my father answered.

"Hitler was a good man for his country, but he went a bit far."

Slapping both hands against the table, Leonhard broke into a broad smile.

"I like you. Fred. I didn't think I could like an Englishman, but I like you."

Maria Eder sighed a massive sigh of relief. Hele looked happy. Everyone did.

"Tell Fred that if I ever get to England, I'm going to find Churchill's grave and put a big pile of stones over it so he can never get out."

This was greeted by a round of laughter. Leonhard raised his right hand and boasted that when he was a member of the Hitler Youth, he once shook hands with the Führer. After watching our faces for reactions, he got up and asked to see the car we had driven. To my father's horror, he stood in front of it with his fists raised. Then, he brought them down on the bonnet of the car, causing it to bounce.

"There. That's why you won the war. Strong English workmanship."

fourteen

Having come to know my way around Währing as well as the more celebrated sights in the city center, I spent a lot of time out on my own. After one afternoon spent exploring, I came back to find emotions in my grandmother's Lacknergasse apartment as ragged and disorderly as the magazines and newspapers strewn across the table.

"What's the matter?"

"Oh nothing," my mother answered.

"There has to be something."

"Oh no, not really," she said, choking back her own words.

Maria Eder looked uncharacteristically stern as my mother started sobbing again and Hele lit another cigarette. Regardless of my appeals to be let in on the secret, I was simply told I was too young to understand. Continued nagging on my part finally squeezed some information out, if only to the extent that "It is something to do with Gerhard." Maybe we ought to get back to the social side of our holiday, I thought, and asked when we were going to see Norbert.

"We won't be seeing Norbert. Not this time."

Days passed. Our time together was marked by sobriety after everyone had taken their chance to celebrate Fred and Leonhard getting along so well after having been on opposite sides in the war. The important thing now was to have everyone on the same side of this new issue. Tears flowed. Words were raised in anger. Newspapers and magazines were studied, so many of them that I couldn't help but slowly work out what had instigated a family crisis.

Those same weekly magazines from which Maria Eder had clipped pictures of Queen Elizabeth and her corgis were printing photographs of her grandson. Now that I had a few facts, I was in a position to ask for more of an explanation. As fragmentary as the answers I received were, they went to the heart of the matter. From my grandmother, mother, Hele, and Leonhard, I heard that "He killed somebody, and now Norbert wants to get a lawyer. Gerhard can be no good anyway. It isn't worth spending money on somebody who would kill an old man like that."

A cloud of shame replaced the clouds of cigarette smoke that were hanging in the room.

fifteen

THE MURDERER OF LEOBERSDORF: so read the caption beneath a two-by-three inch photograph of Gerhard Eder on the front page of the Kurier for May 25th in 1963. For the previous three weeks, there had been a search for the person who had stabbed Milan Popovic, a sixty-one-year-old laborer, and left his body at the edge of a soccer field in the final hour of May Day.

Gerhard began that day in good spirits. He had had an invitation to eat at noon with his girlfriend and her parents. It was a brighter prospect to him than being at home in Neusiedl, where he had spent so many years fetching and carrying and coming home from school with bad reports. Born in 1944, Gerhard found that growing up as the eldest son burdened him with duties such as cleaning house, hauling wood in winter, or even washing the diapers of his youngest siblings. His teacher at school was unaware at first of his circumstances and found no better way of dealing with his wrong answers in class than to cuff him on the ear until he was humiliated. At fourteen, when he left school, his father insisted on what he felt was best and directed him toward an apprenticeship at a mechanic's workshop instead of the building trade, which would have been Gerhard's choice. The apprenticeship was short.

Rather than live at home, Gerhard moved to the Young Workers Village in Hochleiten, not far from Maria Enzersdorf. After breaking curfew too often, he was evicted. During this period, he preferred to spend time in Vienna, and on one occasion, he simply opted not to go to work but to indulge in spontaneous freedom. At other times, he went to visit his uncle, Norbert Eder, where he found a sympathetic companion with whom he could share interests like drawing. Back with Walter, the relationship remained a turbulent one, and after one incident, Gerhard was even sent to an institution for observation for two months. By May Day of 1963, his affairs had taken a calmer course. Not only was he renting a room by himself, he had taken a job as a bricklayer and enjoyed a happier personal life thanks to Helga Sommer and the hospitality of her parents.

Following the midday meal, Gerhard and Helga joined friends at the Gasthaus Stroh in Leobersdorf, situated just to the south of Vienna, for May Day celebrations. They were in high spirits when Milan Popovic appeared. He wanted to play the current hit *Marina, Marina*, and while he was distracted at the jukebox, Gerhard drank the beer Popovic had left on the table. Popovic did not share the joke and left the Gasthaus while the young company laughed on. Next stop for them was the holiday fairground close by. After time spent there, Helga and others felt tired and went home. Gerhard went home too, but he couldn't sleep.

In his room, he had an open bottle of wine, drank that, lay for a while, reflecting on his unruly past and the happy recent changes in his situation. Hungry, he hoped to find the Gasthaus still open so he could get a late snack. The door was locked. He stood wondering what to do. Perhaps there was another place nearby still open. Without warning, Milan Popovic approached him from the darkness, having been sent to pick up some beer by his boss. Gerhard walked away. Popovic followed him. Gerhard wanted to be left alone. Popovic remained insistent.

At eleven o'clock on the morning of May 2nd, Popovic was discovered, still alive but unable to say anything about the person who had stabbed him. Shortly afterwards, he died in hospital. Two hundred Leobersdorf residents were questioned in the following days, including Gerhard. No reason was found to retain any of them. Only one person knew who as responsible. The secret was conveyed to Helga one night when Gerhard leaned close to her while dancing, and after having her promise to tell nobody, confessed.

sixteen

Three weeks later, a knock at Gerhard's door woke him early in the morning. He offered no resistance and maintained he had been afraid to tell anyone what had happened during his confrontation with the older man because he felt nobody would believe his version of events. "There, I started to feel afraid and wanted to avoid an indictment from the Gendarmerie. I dragged the Yugoslav to the nearby meadow, took my pocketknife, and stabbed in the area of the heart. Only when I thought I'd killed him did I stop." Once he had offered his account, he protested that he was not a murderer. As one of the Gendarmes responded with, "We'll tell you what is manslaughter and what is murder."

Gerhard Eder's face was presented in the national press as that of a murderer. The version in the Express showed his eyebrows appearing to have been retouched to create an especially evil effect. None of the Viennese press artists had a brush capable of painting an image of Gerhard equal to the texts that would accompany it. On July 11th, he stared from the front pages again, this time placed next to the innocent face of Brigitte Besztenlerer, and above, these words: "Gerhard Eder was 17 years old when, on February 15. 1961, he murdered the 13-year-old Brigitte Besztenlerer in Maria Enzersdorf. Two-and-a-half years after the deed, he has now confessed."

In black and white, from the authoritative sources of newspapers, and with no trace of doubt, Gerhard was identified as one of the worst individuals imaginable. His grandmother saw no reason to take his side. His aunt and uncle, Hele and Leonhard, saw none. The editors of the Volksblatt saw none either and presented a headline that read, "The crime against Gitti Besztenlerer resolved. The perpetrator is the 'football field murderer.'" In the Kronen Zeitung, Gerhard was described as "An unperson, worse than a vicious wolf, (who) lived among us pretending to be harmless." The report did comment that "Eder doesn't come into question as the

Opera House murderer," and continued with a short reprise of the crime committed in March of 1963 against an eleven-year-old dancer, Dagmar Fuhrich, in Vienna's Opera House. Gerhard's tattoo, dedicated to his cousin, was haunting him. "Unprecedented cheek," the press announced. "After the murder, Eder had Gitti's name tattooed on his arm."

seventeen

The limping man in a leather coat was alluded to in reports but only to back the claim that initial evidence had been deceptive. Josef Jäger, chief reporter in the Kurier, wrote, "Only the ingenuity in matters of crime of the Lower Austrian Gendarmerie officers is to be thanked for the quiet assembly of evidence against Eder that was so indicting that the perpetrator signed a confession following a two-hour interrogation." Jäger listed four points on which to base Gerhard's guilt: He carried knives, sought the company of young girls, lived close to Maria Enzersdorf in February of 1961, and was not at home on the fifteenth. In addition, it was claimed that the manner in which the knife wounds had been inflicted on the thirteen-year-old girl and Milan Popovic were comparable.

"The population can breathe a sigh of relief," announced the Wiener Zeitung. The brothers,

Walter and Norbert Eder, were not as easily persuaded as others in their family that Gerhard was guilty, and each collected copies of every newspaper that carried his story. Here was a photograph of the Young Workers Village where Gerhard had lived, plus one of the sink at which he was supposed to have washed the blood from his hands after committing the crime. And here too was a picture of Gerhard, placed next to a copy of the phantom portrait pieced together by witnesses after Ash Wednesday along with the comment that this was how Eder had appeared to them. In another newspaper, the headline declared that the authorities feared a lynch mob would take the matter into their own hands. Repeatedly, reporters mentioned that Major S.'s team refused to be misled by the reports of the limping man in the leather coat.

"I am finally prepared to offer an unconditional confession of my actions. I did, in fact, engage in sexual relations with Brigitte Besztenlerer of Maria Enzersdorf, and on concluding, acted in such a way as to bring about her death." So began the official confession, signed by Gerhard Eder, which brought a sense of relief to the population in the area around Vienna and disgrace to the young man's family. Only his father and uncle were still not ready to accept what was in the press as true. Norbert wanted to hire a lawyer but was unable to muster the funds himself, so he appealed first to Leonhard and Hele. Asking for help was the last time he spoke to them.

eighteen

Late in 1971, I suddenly decided to move from Manchester to Vienna. As luck would have it, Maria Eder had been moved into a home and felt badly treated by Hele and Leonhard, from whom she expected more support in her twilight years. She had dedicated much of her time to looking after Hele's son Bernhard when they were both at work and trying to earn the money to finish building and setting up the house in Gablitz, west of Vienna.

My parents asked her to move in with them in Manchester. It wasn't an ideal solution, but the best available at the time. As the Lacknergasse apartment had never been given up, it became my first address in Vienna, and I stayed there for almost a year.

My first job was with a company based in the city center producing enamel items, and not long after starting, this Christmas came along with a series of invitations for me from all sides of the family: my aunts Herta and Martha, and of course a special Christmas Eve with Hele and Leonhard, who were as generous as ever with their hospitality. Holidays aside, I often went to eat with Norbert on a weeknight, and Saturday or Sunday would find us on the way, somewhere outside the city.

Something was clearly on Norbert's mind all the time. Little by little, he fed me information on what had happened to Gerhard and showed me all the newspaper reports that had been discussed but never shared with me some eight years previously. I had heard the opinion that Gerhard must be guilty if he had confessed. If he had stabbed an old man, he wasn't worth the effort of helping. It was beyond the imagination of our family circle to consider a statement from official sources or printed in the newspapers as anything but the truth. The family name of Eder brought shame every time it appeared in print. If Gerhard hadn't done what he was accused of, he wouldn't be in prison for it. Years after the first wave of embarrassment, I was hearing another argument, presented as if Norbert's apartment were a courtroom.

To emphasize the political aspect of the case, he stressed the award of seven thousand Austrian Schillings to each of the Gendarmerie officers who had worked to solve it. Opening up a page from the Arbeiter Zeitung, dated July 16th, 1963, Norbert circled with his finger a picture of the officers wearing their best suits as they were presented to the Minister for the Interior, Franz Olah, who ceremoniously thanked them for their diligence: "What brings us together today is appreciation for an effort which is no exception, but which should be recognized. It was accomplished in the selfless expedition of obligations of executive duty and is especially to be emphasized at a time in which all—even the executive—are facing criticism." Here was an award given within days of the confession and long before a trial, accompanied by a speech carefully worded to pacify a public impatient at the failure to resolve one of a series of sex-related murders.

Little by little, page by page, a document at a time, I received an education in what had happened to Gerhard from the moment the Gendarmerie officers first considered the tattoo on his arm as a sign that he had killed Brigitte Besztenlerer. The tattoo reference eventually disappeared as evidence, but I was being introduced to the way official Austria worked as uncomfortable details filtered through to the public. Once Gerhard's guilt had been widely proclaimed, Lower Austria's Security Director, Martin Schobel, issued a statement: "The Security Direction was informed unofficially that the court medical examinations so far have been negative and therefore, the murder confession of Gerhard Eder, 19, is to be strongly doubted. Eder could never be the murderer."

Shortly after this, the province's Governor Figl wrote to Minister Olah: "As Governor of the largest province, I should expect that even the Federal Minister for the Interior would not make important decisions such as the one of which I was informed in writing on October 2nd, 1963, without first coming to an agreement with me."

Claiming that public security in the province had been suffering due to questions of jurisdiction, Olah dismissed Martin Schobel and the head of the Criminal Police Department. This happened while Gerhard sat in jail and his trial while still more than a year away. The press and the public could only have seen the proceedings as a formality.

nineteen

Norbert had been doing more than collecting and analyzing newsprint. When I asked whether I could go with him to visit Gerhard in the prison at Stein, he told me he had no intention of going there again until he had found the actual perpetrator. This had become his obsession. He thought about it constantly. When I called him, he said I should never talk about what we discussed and over the telephone only refer to "The Case," never mentioning names. Meanwhile, whenever we went out, he first set up a little device with a string and a light bulb at the base of his apartment door, stopping to adjust it by bending down and slipping his hand inside once he'd gone into the hallway. This, he said, was so he would know should anyone enter his home while he was away.

Once out on the street, I noticed that he had taken to looking behind him ever more

frequently. His behavior suggested an explanation for the black hair dye I immediately noticed
when he first met me at the railway station. Was
he trying to look young? I wondered. Was this
an attempt at disguise?

One evening, as we leaned back in our
wooden seats at a Gasthaus near Ruckergasse,
Norbert looked carefully around while he wiped
his lips with a napkin, then leaned forward and
spoke quietly.

"The Gendarmerie called me again last week."

"Do they do this often?" I asked.

"Oh, once a year usually."

"So, what did they want?"

"The officer had me come in and sit down.
He was very proper. He just asked whether I'd
made any progress with my work."

"What did you tell him?"

"I told him the truth, that I hadn't found a
new perpetrator."

"How did he react to that?"

"He just said that made him very happy."

On another evening, realizing how obsessive
this undertaking had become for him, Norbert

suggested a film for a diversion. We chose *Death in Venice*. During the scene in the film with Aschenbach gazing out to the sea from a deck chair with a bead of sweat carrying black dye from his hair down his face, I glanced to my right at Norbert. He shifted in his seat, reacting to the onscreen image of a man who could have been his double. As I could see the discomfort in Norbert's face, I felt a flush of embarrassment for both of us run through me.

twenty

Placing a copy of Stern magazine in front of me, Norbert slapped the open page. "You remember who Alfred Knotek was, don't you? In a new trial for Gerhard, he would have been the main witness, the last one to see Gitti alive. He died in 1969, in a car crash. Knotek was the one person who saw the man in the leather coat follow her. The accident happened in March, and the possible reopening of the case was still making news. It was a head on crash with a taxi in Wiener Neudorf. Knotek was twenty-two then. Not long after this was printed in the paper, I had someone tell me they saw a person tampering with Knotek's car beforehand. The main witness, dead." Whether Knotek's death had been a coincidence or the result of a plot made no difference to the impact it had on Norbert. Having grown quiet again, he turned to our next project: Renee H.

On a Sunday afternoon in springtime, we strolled along a village street talking about films currently showing in Vienna. It felt good to leave the murder story behind and enjoy the quiet place. I realized that we were in this particular spot by design when, as we passed a particular address, Norbert directed his gaze downward and spoke in a quiet voice. "The lady who lives there telephoned me last week. She had read about my work on the case and wanted me to know about a renter she had been staying here in 1961. She said the man made her nervous and remembered that about the time of the Fog Murder, he had her take his leather coat to the cleaner. One day, he invited her to drink a glass of red wine with her, and when he opened a drawer in his room to take the corkscrew out, she saw a long knife that made her worry for herself. He limped. He fit the description of the man they were looking for, absolutely. His name was Renee H."

Having given me time to absorb the importance of what the lady had said, Norbert arranged for me to go and see him again on the next Wednesday. I found him at home, working at a table covered with photographs, one of which he handed to me. It showed a grave marked with the family name of his newest discovery. "We have a long way to go," Norbert said, "to Steyr. Renee H. died some years ago. I looked up his records. A brother there is his one surviving relative. Now, this is what we need to do. You make a nice folder for the picture, something that shows you think it is special. Then, we're going to see this brother. We have to find out all we can about Renee. To do that, we need a reason to get in and talk to the brother and his wife. You will show the folder with the photograph and tell him you came to Austria from England and wanted to look up the man who once saved your father's life. That was Renee H. Say he was working on a project that concerned the British army—maybe it had to do with railways. So, your father wanted you to find this man, but you learned that he is dead and went to visit his grave. You intend to take the picture back to your father in England and want to be able to tell him all about this man, Renee H."

To make our journey even more relevant, it was set for November 1st, the day to remember the dead. The weather turned out to be appropriately mysterious. After the ritual of setting up the alarm system across the threshold of his apartment, Norbert strode out toward his car. All the way from Vienna to Upper Austria, we traveled through fog. When we turned off the motorway and onto country roads, I was fascinated by the shapes of the farmhouses resembling huge animals crouched in the grainy atmosphere. Just before noon, we entered Steyr, with the buildings of its famous main square barely visible. Norbert checked the address written on a sheet of paper and wound down his window to ask one of the few pedestrians for directions. The address was for an apartment block, which we found easily. A serious expression signaled Norbert's tension while I felt more relaxed about our adventure, as if it were just another of our excursions and not a detective mission. We were able to enter the house by the street door and walked past the elevator shaft to the ground floor apartment.

"I'll ring the bell, and then you step forward with the picture and introduce yourself when it opens."

I wondered for a second why we hadn't found a telephone number and called it ahead of our visit to be sure someone would be at home to meet us after our two-hour drive. The door opened slightly. I felt the heat escaping from inside the apartment and could see a man and a woman, close together, peering curiously out at their unannounced visitors. My initial greeting was quickly followed by, "and I wanted to meet the brother of Renee H., who once saved…" My sentence was cut short at the slamming of the door. We stared at each other, not knowing what the rebuff signified, and went away to eat lunch at the first open restaurant we could find. Neither of us had anything to say other than Norbert's "They can only have acted that way if they knew there is something to hide."

twenty-one

"Shitty bunch, all of you." As he spat the words, Norbert opened a newspaper from his archive and went on to describe Gerhard's outburst during his trial when he realized the extent to which he had been lied to. Piecemeal, I had received isolated details of the story, and while much remained a mystery to me, I was in no doubt of Gerhard's innocence. Despite his increasingly nervous behavior, Norbert was convincing, and I still admired what he was doing to try and find the limping man in the leather coat.

Having thought more as weeks passed about Renee H., Norbert told me he believed that he could not have been the Fog Murderer. He didn't elaborate on why but went on to describe another telephone call he had received.

"A woman got in touch with me to say she thinks her husband could be the man who has killed a number of victims. She observed that each time a murder involving a young woman occurred, he was working in the area where it happened. Once, there was a killing in Graz, and her husband's firm had a contract there exactly at the time. With all this background, she has ceased to believe in coincidence. Something about his manner disturbs her, especially when the weather changes for the worse. I met her last week, and she thinks I should find a way to see him. He was even working near the Opera House when a girl was murdered there. She suggested I try to meet her husband, and she will know who we are when we visit."

We planned another evening at the cinema, this time to see Last Tango in Paris. After eating out, we still had plenty of time before the showing began, and as the cinema was in the city center, I suggested we use the hour to have Norbert meet my friend Franz Moser, who lived not far away. Norbert and Franz were as different as two men could be, my uncle having been a man of the city, while Franz came from a village in Carinthia. He had moved to Vienna to study art. The walls of his apartment were covered with his paintings, some figurative, some abstract. Perhaps they would enjoy each other's company after all, I thought, and Franz lived close to where we would be going.

While Franz brought out a bottle of something strong and clear, fresh from his home province, Norbert looked around at the artwork. We took one drink apiece and chatted inconsequentially. Anna Moser came into the room and introduced herself. Norbert asked what her profession was.

"I am a psychiatrist."

After showing us a few more paintings that were as yet unframed, Franz offered another drink. We declined, having by now to get back to the cinema.

The rest of our evening ran its course. I couldn't tell whether Norbert liked Marlon Brando's performance or whether he had even taken much notice of it. We made plans to meet on Saturday for our latest mission. Before going home, I asked Norbert what he thought of Franz Moser's paintings. His facial expression showed he was uncomfortable. "They are too bright, too gaudy for my taste," he said. "I don't like them at all."

twenty-two

Norbert had the plan for our Saturday morning worked out. He drove us out to a district where the grey of the buildings was interrupted by a few small garden plots. In winter, they too were without color. In one of them, a man was working behind a fence. We wandered toward him and tried to appear as though we were lost. Norbert called to the man to ask for help and explained that we were looking for a particular street. The name he had chosen was one for which there was no street, a ploy to guarantee a long search and more time with this stranger.

We were invited back to the man's home, where he said he had a map. Once inside the overheated apartment, we sat down and waited while the man's wife, who had already met Norbert, went to make us a hot drink. Meanwhile, the man went to change from his outdoor clothing into shorts and to fetch his street map. He returned, sat down, and gestured for his daughter, who looked to be about twelve, to come and sit on his lap. We stayed for about twenty minutes and left, feigning disappointment that our street had not been located. Walking back to his car, Norbert commented that the face of the man was close enough to the phantom portrait created back in 1961. I had noticed his complexion, which was distinctly pockmarked. We went our separate ways after arranging an appointment at the National Library for the coming week. We planned to look through newspaper archives for reports from various murders.

Norbert had ordered back issues of newspapers in advance, so all we had to do was collect them from the main desk before sitting down at a table in the Austrian National Library. I had previously walked up the steps of this imposing nineteenth century building to visit its collections of musical instruments and art from exotic places and had toured the elaborate rooms of the Habsburgs. On this evening, the history that interested us was between twelve and fifteen years into the past. We had resolved to study reports of those murders which concerned us, and I picked the Opera House case to look into, while across the table from me, Norbert sat peering through his glasses at information that was already familiar to him. We hoped for any small detail that might inspire a new idea.

Dagmar Fuhrich, a budding ballet dancer, was twelve years old on the afternoon she was assaulted and killed inside the Opera House following a rehearsal. The man we had recently been to visit had been, according to his wife, working for a company that had a contract at the Opera House at the time of this murder. As I ran my finger under line after line of newsprint, I suddenly felt a shiver run directly from the paper through my arm and along my spine when I read a quote from a witness who had seen a man cross the Ringstraße just after the time of Dagmar's death. The man was obviously in a hurry, and the one identifying feature the witness focused on was his pockmarked face. I slid the newspaper over to Norbert. He read the passage and immediately began to fold away the rest of the newspapers he had before him.

We went our separate ways. I went home on the number 71 tram after Norbert had walked away in the direction of his car. That was the last time I ever saw him.

twenty-three

Two weeks passed without me receiving a telephone call from Norbert. I dialed his number from the booth on Simmeringer Hauptstraße, where I lived, and we talked briefly. He said he was busy and had no time for us to get together right now. Similar conversations took place a couple of times before I decided to stop calling and wait until Norbert contacted me. Months went by. At my workplace, the design studio of a large soap detergent company, I talked about this turn of events with my colleagues. The studio head knew all about my adventures with Norbert and seemed to be good judge of character. "Your uncle's just trying to protect you," he said, "and obviously thinks there is some danger." This was the explanation I accepted during the winter and early springtime. As the trees were coming into blossom and the sky was brightening, an envelope arrived at my mailbox with my address in familiar handwriting. I knew it was from Norbert, but there was no message inside, just a page from an old weekend issue of the Kronen Zeitung's magazine supplement. Immediately I recognized it as the questionnaire that had long rested inside the glove compartment of Norbert's car. Puzzled, I showed the envelope and contents to my boss. His face lit up. "He wants to get back in touch with you."

This made sense. Norbert had always been fond of quiet jokes. I looked up the number for the Paul Zsolnay publishing company, dialed, and asked the receptionist to connect me with Herr Eder.

"Eder."

"Yes, Herr Eder," I began in an artificially formal voice, "I would like to ask whether the questionnaire ought to be returned by mail, or perhaps I should bring it in person."

Several seconds of silence were followed by, "David, get off my back. Why did we go to the Mosers that night anyway?"

Late in the summer, another communication reached me: a postcard mailed in Barcelona bearing a photograph of a large monkey. The scribbles masquerading as handwriting told me something about looking in the mirror. Close to this time, I heard from another family member that Norbert had sent something to Walter Eder as well, which was a parcel of excrement.

twenty-four

Without Norbert, I had neither the resources nor the inclination to keep up with Gerhard's case. I was not in touch with Walter Eder, the only person who kept up with any new developments. By the time I left Vienna to live in Arizona in 1978, I didn't know where Gerhard's story had ended, only that he had served his sentence and been released.

The first time I returned to Vienna in 1983, I heard that Norbert had died. There was no news of where he had lived, and the date of his death must have been around 1980. All his work on Gerhard's behalf had left me with the unanswered questions of why the confession had been made and who the actual Fog Murderer had been. In April of 1994, I made my third return trip to Vienna since leaving, having resolved to learn how the trial of an innocent person had resulted in his being convicted and to find the name of the man who had killed Gitti Besztenlerer.

Walter Eder hadn't been expecting to hear from a nephew he hadn't seen for a long time, but he sounded enthusiastic, if a little weak, when he answered my phone call made after I arrived in Vienna. In April of that year, he was in poor health, and I didn't know he only had a year to live. I found him sitting outside his house in Neusiedl-am-See, enjoying the sunlight.

"I'll get a bottle of wine. I know I shouldn't, but my doctor would forgive me for a special visit."

He opened a double-liter bottle of red wine. We spent some time talking about our respective lives and current projects before I mentioned how much I'd thought about Gerhard since my experiences with Norbert. Walter had nothing bad to say about his brother and offered no more than a sad smile as he reflected on the story, while I said, "I often wondered who the murderer was."

Walter sat quietly. He looked up and told me, "I used to have all the newspaper clippings. They must be in the house somewhere, but I don't know where. Besides, I think I'd have to move a lot of furniture to get at them. If I come across them, I'll let you know."

"I'll move any furniture you have to get at them now," I quickly replied.

My trip wasn't planned as a long one. In less than two weeks, I would be back in Phoenix. What I had expected to be doing for much of my time in Vienna was sitting in the reading room of the National Library, where I'd last seen Norbert, reading whatever I could find based on the dates I knew.

"Well, let's go in and have a look."

The box Walter needed was in the first room we looked in, and I had very little furniture to move in the process of getting hold of it. Inside a large carton were the scrapbooks and neatly arranged copies of documents. I took stock of the contents while we sat talking and sipping red wine in front of the house. Here were many of the newspapers I recalled from Norbert's collection with photographs that were strangely familiar to me, although I hadn't seen them in twenty years. There was Gerhard standing in the courtroom, Gerhard illuminated by the ghost-lights of Scheidpark at night, Gerhard's arm bearing the tattoo, and one picture I had never seen before of Walter giving Gerhard a bouquet of roses as he met him on his release from the prison at Stein. One news clipping also had a new picture for me, a picture of a white glove illustrating an article about new clues in the Ilona Faber case. It reminded me that although Norbert had shown me the glove, he never went into any detail as to why he had it. My assumption had been that he was simply so engrossed in serial killings that he was likely to collect anything linked to them. It was all part of the passion that burned him up.

"Where is Gerhard now?"

"We don't know exactly. He's somewhere in Vienna," Walter said.

"I'd like to read through these. Can I borrow them for a few days? I promise you'll have them back soon."

twenty-five

As part of an article written by Ernst Ebm, I found the map that showed the route taken by Ilona Faber's murderer on his way from Schwarzenbergpark. With this as my guide, I started out at the spot where the story really began and took my walk into a vignette of Viennese history.

During a long session at a photocopy shop, I made four hundred and fifty copies. This was Walter's complete collection. Luckily for me, he had been thorough. The only missing chapters were those concerned with Ilona Faber's murder, an event he had no particular reason to follow at the time it happened. This omission was easily rectified at the Library. Now, I had a mass of printed material in which I found names familiar to me from the time I had spent with Norbert: the auto dealer Hans Luksch, Detective Walter Jaromin, and reporter Ernst Ebm.

With three names, a mug of coffee, and the Vienna telephone directory, I sat down and began dialing people with the names Luksch, Jaromin, and Ebm.

"Hello Herr Luksch. Is it possible that you are the Luksch who found the blood in..."

The voices on the answering machines I reached sounded too young.

"Herr Luksch. I am researching the case of Brigitte Besztenlerer."

Click. The recipient of my call hung up. So much for Luksch. Neither in Vienna nor in Perchtoldsdorf did I find Hans Luksch, so I moved on to Jaromin. Walter Jaromin had been a private detective. My attempts to reach him met with the same results as my search for Hans Luksch had. I didn't feel very optimistic when I turned to Ebm, but there was one entry for an Ernst Ebm. The name was right. Why not try?

"Hello, Herr Ebm? Do you happen to be the reporter who wrote about Gerhard Eder some years ago?"

"Yes."

"I am Eder's cousin, visiting from the United States. I'm trying to research his case to find out who committed that murder."

"Of course, I remember the case. Come right over. I always wished somebody would take an interest in that boy."

After a short walk beside the Danube Canal along Schüttelstrasee, with trees to my left and dull grey walls to my right, I arrived at Ernst Ebm's address. He welcomed me enthusiastically and gave me a summary tour of his apartment, apologizing for the untidy state of his rooms but pointing out the quality of the Biedermeier paintings that hung in them.

"I spent a lot of time with Norbert Eder," I told him, "and always knew that Gerhard was not guilty of the Fog Murder."

"Norbert got many things wrong."

"When Gerhard was first arrested, nobody in the family would tell me more than they absolutely had to."

Ebm replied that he wasn't surprised and that he found the family altogether strange. Leonhard Brand wouldn't even grant him an interview.

"He was a piece of work," Ebm mused.

"He always insisted that if Gerhard killed one man, he wasn't worth helping anyway," I said. "I have just come across information among papers I got from Walter Eder that indicates the Popovic case was manslaughter and not murder, so Leonhard's attitude was especially hard for me to accept."

Ebm stood up. "Manslaughter!" He raised his right arm as if holding an object in preparation of bringing it down on my head. "What would you do if someone came up behind you in the dark with a broken bottle, ready to attack you with it? It was self defense, pure and simple."

We drank some tea while Ebm told me he had been a translator at the Nuremberg trials before coming back to Vienna to work as a reporter.

"Norbert tried to do what he could," I offered.

"Yes, but he got it all wrong."

I mentioned our adventures together and my strange introduction to the story when I was shown the long white glove.

"We gave him that along with some other things when we had finished with them," Ebm said.

"I've been able to read how the confession came about, but I want to know who did kill Brigitte Besztenlerer."

Without a second's hesitation or any hint of doubt, Ebm exclaimed, "Josef Reinhard. It was absolutely clear. I worked with Luksch and Jaromin when the trial was over, and we came up with conclusive evidence. Everything fit, every detail was right in place."

As Ebm backed up his conclusion with a few observations from his work as an investigative reporter, I made a few notes. Then, he stood and led me toward his door, where he picked up a skull from a table.

"During the time I was working on the case, I came home one day to find this outside my door along with a note telling me that if I didn't stop what I was doing, I'd end up like this. Of course, it made no difference to me. I carried on anyway."

Before I left, he asked me to wait while he pulled some photographs from his files. These were pictures I had seen over the past couple of days among the newspaper articles I had borrowed from Walter. "Take these," he said, "and use them however you like."

Ersnt Ebm shows me the skull
left at his door as a warning (1993)

twenty-six

After having a couple of days to read and absorb material from Walter Eder's collection of papers, I was back with Ernst Ebm, who was happy to have someone with whom he could relive a story that still meant so much to him.

What I already knew was why Gerhard had given a confession in the first place. He gave an account of what had happened to him in custody long after the fact, and it was reproduced in the body of an article published in the Echo on December 7th, 1969, under the headline "I am not the Fog Murderer!" and compiled by a writer named Peter Hatheyer.

To outsiders, Gerhard acknowledged at the outset that this story may seem absurd but that outsiders have not been in the position in which Gerhard had found himself when officers first confronted him and asked him why he thought he was being interrogated.

"What about the incident with Gitti? How was that?"

Gerhard was taken aback by the question and shook his head.

"Maria Enzersdorf."

He remembered that a girl had been murdered there two years previously but didn't know why this was being mentioned. Without receiving an answer, the Gendarmes questioning him took him back to his cell. A month later, he was back in the interrogation room.

"Well, we've had you brought here because we didn't want to lose contact with you. There is a reason we want to talk to you. Think about it."

"What should I think about? What I done, I confessed to. That's why I'm 'ere."

"Think on. We are of the opinion that you have something else on your account."

"I dunno. I know nothin'."

After being left alone for half an hour, Gerhard was taken to his cell, where he waited for three more weeks before the Gendarmes returned to begin their questions over again.

"Well, have you thought about it? About what it could be?"

"What 'ave I got to think about?"

"Just think back. Think again. You know, we haven't brought you here for fun."

Once again, Gerhard was left alone for a while before being led back to his cell, where he waited until June 9th, 1963, when he was writing a letter. At three o'clock in the afternoon, Inspectors Fe., Fo., and Z. arrived and asked him to get dressed and go with them. Beginning with inconsequential chat, the inspectors asked how Gerhard was feeling.

"'ow can I be getting' on in clink?"

Inspector Fe. was first to come to the point.

"How about this? How was it that time, February 15th, fog, Gitti?"

"Whaddaya want o' me? I've got nothin' to do with that thing. Weren't me."

Z. raised his voice to a scream.

"What are you thinking about? That you can treat us as if we were stupid? We've got witnesses to you being at the cinema. We have witnesses who saw you at the scene of the crime. They can testify in court, testify to all that."

"That's impossible 'cause I weren't in no cinema, neither were I there when it were done."

"Sure. You may think others are stupid. Not us!"

"I've nothin' to do wi' that. I can't say nothin' else about it."

"If you admit to it now, you know, well first, the judge has an easier time at the trial, doesn't he? And there will certainly be an audience in the courtroom, and you would, let's see, get maybe ten years, and with a third of that taken off, that leaves seven years. Well, seven years is what you'll get anyway with the murder you've already got to answer for. What's more, trials cost the kind of money you don't have."

For the next seven hours, variations on the same questions continued. Only when Inspector B. joined his colleagues was there a break in the harangue. He addressed Gerhard in a friendly tone, offering him cigarettes. Inspector Fe. came back to the central theme.

"Now Gerhard, how was it that time with the girl? You killed her, didn't you?"

Z. raised the decibel level once more.

"It's easy to think you can treat us as if we were stupid. That takes somebody other than you. Admit it. We have proof. We have witnesses who can say they saw you there and will tell the court it was you who killed the girl. You were in the cinema. You were even seen there!"

Gerhard felt desperate to explain that he could not have been seen in the cinema when he was not there, but he couldn't find the words. He was no longer sure of anything by eleven o'clock at night, but he grasped at the memory of an alibi: the man he said gave him a ride on his motorcycle. A Hungarian. Domboru was his name. Silvester Domboru. Z. cut the claim short with another scream.

"Every word you say is a lie because it is not true you got a ride. You were observed at the scene of the murder, and you were in the cinema!"

Z.'s shouting alternated with the fatherly voice of B., who told Gerhard that if he helped the Gendarmes now, they would help him in court when he faced a judge and jury with the press and members of the public present. One murder or two. He couldn't deny killing Milan

Popovic, and this was his chance for leniency. In court, he was told, the pressure would build just as it did for the Nazi Eichmann, and Gerhard would surely break. Gerhard wanted nothing but to lie down and sleep and finally summoned the energy to tell his interrogators that if they really thought they knew everything better than he did, then he did do whatever they were accusing him of. The two-hour interrogation that was cited in a newspaper report at the time the confession was announced had lasted at least nine hours until Inspector B. asked Gerhard what he would like to eat now that it was so late at night, a Wiener Schnitzel perhaps? Yes, that will be fine, a piece of pork, beaten and dipped in flour, egg, and bread-crumbs, then deep fried. The friendly Gendarme called out for the midnight meal.

twenty-seven

Once the plate had been cleared away, Gerhard could still not look forward to sleep. There was paperwork to be done. A confession had to be recorded in detail if it was to be credible. How had the girl been dragged into the park? How much of a struggle had taken place? Believing it to be in his own interest to provide this account, Gerhard prepared to describe the murder with a typist waiting to record what he had to say.

Fe. asked how the girl had defended herself. Gerhard made a guess, drawing on whatever he remembered from newspaper reports published two years previously. How was the body positioned? Gerhard's answer didn't fit in with the facts, so Z. pointed out which direction she must have been facing. Gerhard changed his answer. His corrected version was duly noted. Z. wanted to know whether the girl was raped. Gerhard denied that he raped her.

"Why not, all of a sudden, when it is all so clear that you are the perpetrator!"

Gerhard then said that he did rape her. Now to the actual killing: how often did he stab her? Twice. How had the wounds been delivered? Through her clothes. By the time the confession was ready to be signed, it was not a document written in Gerhard's rough colloquial German but in the most correct language.

"I am finally prepared to offer an unconditional confession of my actions. I did, in fact, engage in sexual relations with Brigitte Besztenlerer of Maria Enzersdorf, and on concluding, acted in such a way as to bring about her death."

A passage followed in which Gerhard stated that he had known Brigitte Besztenlerer and was an enthusiastic film viewer, eager to watch whatever was shown.

"I liked Brigitte Besztenlerer very much, which is to say I found her very attractive. Therefore, I wished that I could eventually engage in relations with her. I understand by this that I could at some time have sex with her.

"I knew Brigitte Besztenlerer only by the first name of Gitti, which I came to be aware of through other people calling her by this name.

"On 15 February 1961, I traveled from the building site in the eighth district of Vienna by tram to Maria Enzersdorf. After work ended at 17.00, I took the tram to Maria Enzersdorf and arrived toward 17.45 at the Kirchengasse stop. I walked from the stop in the direction of the church as far as the Hauptstraße, then turned right until I reached the bus stop, which is near a Gasthaus. Among us boys, this was called *To Hell* and is in fact named *Gasthaus of the Black Eagle*. I usually drank beer and did so at this Gasthaus. I sat alone at a table, but other customers were present. I can still recall that there was a heavy fog. In my opinion, I only drank one glass of beer, but I must honestly admit that I cannot be sure of the exact amount I consumed. I can also no longer say whether I spoke with anyone in the Gasthaus. I had the intention of going home to the Young Workers Village in Hochleiten.

"At the bus stop close by, I stayed for a while in the shelter. I think that I had spent about

1½ hours in the Gasthaus of the Black Eagle. As I went to the bus stop shelter, there must have been a waiting time of about 30 minutes. It was often my habit to stand and wait to see whether I would meet an acquaintance there.

"After several people with whom I was not familiar walked by me, I gathered that the film showing was over. This was undoubtedly the first of the evening's showings, which in general are over between seven-thirty and eight pm. Finally, I could see that a girl was walking along the path through the park behind the bus shelter. She walked along the pavement on the main street past me as I waited in the bus shelter. I recognized this girl as the previously indicated Gitta, but she took no notice of me. I do not even think that she recognized me.

"I let the girl go about 20 meters ahead of me and set off after her with the intention of getting closer to her. By this, I mean that I wanted to screw her.

"After Gitta went forward with a quick step, I moved even more quickly after her. On the right side of the pavement, I walked beside the park to the street corner where a cross-street branches to the right, leading toward Gießhübl. At this street corner, I grabbed hold of Gitta with the firm intention of raping her."

The ensuing paragraphs detail the choreography of grabbing the girl and placing a hand across her mouth to silence her, followed by Gerhard claiming to have known the concrete foundation from previous walks through the park and thinking of it as a good place for the sex act.

"It was absolutely dark, and I could only perceive the girl's outline. During this entire activity, my member became stiff, and I had the definite intention 'of screwing her.' Because Gitta wanted to scream again, I took my handkerchief out of the right pocket of my trousers with my right hand, took it in my left hand, and with this, I held Gitta's mouth shut."

The complex maneuvers of sex are chronicled next, followed by the rationale that led Gerhard to kill the girl.

"During the entire activity, I had Gitta's forearms crossed on her chest, and I pushed these with my left forearm against her neck so that she could hardly move.

"I was now afraid that Gitta would tell her mother about the assault and that she would report me, resulting in my being officially accused. In order to prevent this, I took out my pocket-knife (this was about as long as my index finger, had black panels on the sides of the handle, and on each side at the point of maximum width was a metal ornament in the shape of an arrowhead) with my right hand, opened the blade using my left thumb and index finger, all the time continuing to hold Gitta down. With my right hand, I then guided the knife and stabbed Gitta. I can still remember two stabs. I stabbed her once in the breast and once in the lower body. It was very dark then, and I could see almost nothing. It is also possible that I stabbed more often."

The pocketknife was folded and wiped with a handkerchief, a colored one from home, after the girl's death-rattle sounds. The description of Gerhard leaving the park began with him looking for and picking up the duffle bag he had let go of.

"I ran through the park in the direction of the street along which the tram goes. There were bushes and an old fence. This fence was torn down in some places, while in others, it was as high as my chest. At one of the torn sections, I was able to get onto the street. There, I looked around to see whether anyone was coming. Seeing nobody, I went out and onto the street. I ran as far as a Gasthaus on the right side, opposite the castle. From there, I walked quickly. I hardly had the breath to run anymore. I saw nobody."

The final page is concerned with the arrival back at the Young Workers Village and going to the washroom sink to clean up clothes and the pocketknife.

This text did not fit comfortably with what was already known. Gerhard referred throughout to the victim as Gitta rather than Gitti. Would he have used the name of his cousin in France over and over even if he had misspoken once? If Gerhard had been the person scrambling through the fence at the edge of the park by the automobile driver, wouldn't the driver have noticed him carrying the duffle bag? Twice, the tracker dogs had followed the perpetrator's scent to the tram stop where it ended. If Gerhard had run and walked all the way home, the scent would have continued. Nobody is mentioned wearing a leather coat. The man who got on the number 360 tram had suddenly disappeared. Had he been innocently waiting for the tram would he have seen the escaping murderer?

Two days later, dated July 11th, a further section was added to the confession:

"With every respect to peace and decorum, The Investigative Judge has explained to me the implications of the confession and the senselessness of giving a false confession, and I hereby indicate that this confession has been made by me without any form of persuasion or force whatsoever."

twenty-eight

Walter Eder was the first to publicly express doubt toward the confession. "Only when he looks me in the eye and admits to committing this crime will I believe him," he told a Kronen Zeitung reporter. Meanwhile, Walter continued to assemble his extensive collection of news reports on his son's case, no matter how painful reading accounts of Gerhard's childhood were to him. An issue of Wiener Samstag, an independent weekly, ran an article in which Gerhard's former landlady said of her tenant:

"He didn't like work. When he saw a girl, he dropped everything and ran after her. In winter, he didn't earn much, and I often gave him breakfast free. He didn't want to go home. He didn't get on with his parents. He told how awful they had been to him. He drank too. Often, he got home late, and when he once needed money, he sold his old moped for two hundred Schillings."

In the following paragraph, an aunt of Gerhard's has only good words for him, as she tells how she was the first to send a care packet to him in Wiener Neustadt, containing cigarettes.

"He was my favorite child, my favorite nephew. He was treated badly at home. The child was always being pulled between his mother and grandmother. He wasn't afraid of work, certainly not. He always worked hard. His mother is to blame for all this. She harmed him, and his father ought to have reported it. Gerhard is just a step-child. He counted for nothing among his siblings."

When he pasted this article into his scrap book, Walter underlined the aunt's comments in colored ink.

twenty-nine

Friday, July 26th, 1963. Two am. Artificial lights
create a ghostly setting at the Sheidpark for the
on-site reconstruction of the crime, as required
when a party has admitted to committing it. This
was a performance starring the accused and a
life-size dummy representing Gitti Besztenlerer,
dressed in the clothes she wore as she was murdered. Some photographers were allowed to take
pictures showing Gerhard in a pale sports jacket
and dark slacks, holding his inert stand-in victim.
Only the spot at which Gitti was killed was left in
dim light to better replicate the original conditions.

Lower Austria's Security director, Martin
Schobel, oversaw the event. His primary duty was
to ensure Gerhard's safety with a hundred men
under his direction to guard against the lynch
mob mood that threatened to take action. Dr. S.,
the judge responsible for the pre-trial investigation, was in charge. State attorney Dr. Josef Z. and

medical examiner Dr. Leopold Breitenecker were also present and taking notes. Kuno and Witty, the police dogs, wagged their tails. Reporters were not invited. The dogs' job was to see they were kept at bay and that nobody infiltrated by climbing one of the trees. One journalist who had followed the case in detail was Ernst Ebm. He went to Maria Enzersdorf that night and stayed close to the fringe of events.

At the point where the girl was supposed to have been first lifted from the pavement, Gerhard, adjusting his duffle bag, picked up the dummy and tried to describe what happened. His comments were recorded for the official protocol, reflecting his broad dialect.

"Gitti was 'ardly able to move because of my grip. I mean that the body, with exception of her limbs, was unable to move. She tried to defend 'erself, but I can't remember exactly how."

Dr. Breitenecker asked, "Did she grab your hair, did she try to reach your face with her free hand?"

"Gitti reached toward me 'ead with 'er right 'and but couldn't reach me face or 'air. Other than that, it didn't bother me."

At the corner of Johannesgasse, Gerhard steered the dummy toward the park and said, "I didn't see a path at first. I just come across this one."

Dr. S.: "What did you intend? Did you want to have sex with her?"

"Yeah, first I wanted into the park so I wouldn't be seen. I came up with the idea of going to the concrete foundation, through the fog, because the grass was wet."

When he reached the spot, an official photographer recorded the moment.

Dr. Breitenecker: "Did the girl bite?"

"No, I weren't 'urt at all."

Dr. S.: "Did Gitti still have her coat on at the base of the foundation?"

"I think Gitti still 'ad 'er coat on 'ere. Whether the coat was open or buttoned at the beginnin' I dunno. Whether Gitti still 'ad 'er coat on later I dunno anymore. I know nothin' about 'er gloves."

Gerhard placed the dummy with the body parallel to the Hauptstrasse and the head pointing toward Johannesgasse.

"I now put Gitti down on her left side and shifted my grip to my left 'and, without freeing 'er mouth for very long. At the switch, she gave a very short cry, what it was I don't know anymore. Whether Gitti still 'ad 'er coat on I don't know. I tried to turn Gitti onto 'er back. Gitti tried to stop me."

The next photograph was taken with the dummy as Gerhard went on to offer a complex description of his hand movements as he struggled to negotiate a position. At the crucial moment, Gerhard broke down and began to cry. The official photographers ceased taking pictures until he regained his composure.

"Whether the stockins were still in place, I dunno. I do remember that I looked for 'er pants and found 'em. I dunno details any more. I didn't talk to her. Naturally, she wasn't in agreement with what was 'appening. I still pulled her panties off."

Gerhard gave short answers to the judge's questions during the most intimate events. While Gerhard fumbled with the dummy, Dr. S. asked, "What did you do next?"

"Up to now, I 'ad no intention of doin' 'er in. I only wanted to screw 'er. Now, I was afraid and was nervous too 'cause she peraps knew me and where I live. Then I took the knife out. The knife was closed.

I reached into me coat pocket and took the knife out. I stabbed twice… If it was more often, I dunno."

Looking around for an escape route, Gerhard indicated a path through the park. "Whether the path forked after ten meters, I don't know anymore. I 'eard no sound from round about. In the park, it was silent."

He explained that he intended to avoid Johannesgasse so as not to be seen and reached Helferstorferstraße through the fence. From here, he said he went off on foot to the Young Workers Village. The proceedings moved back to the bus stop where Gerhard said he had been waiting to show how he initially followed the girl and to establish that she had recognized him. After this phase came further questions. Asked how he knew her name was Gitti, he said it was from her friends calling after her. Whether she was ever known as Gitta, Gerhard claimed not to know.

Dr. Breitenecker was comparing what he saw with his findings from 1961 when he examined the body. He asked specific questions relating to the way Gerhard had held the girl and the nature of her struggle.

Dr. Z. asked why Gerhard put the dummy down about nine feet from where the body was found and continued, "Did you, when you stabbed her, stab into the naked body?"

"Through 'er clothes."

Dr. Breitenecker was puzzled. He recalls finding the girl's pullover pushed up above her chest and the knife wounds that had been made directly into her bare flesh. He asked, "Did you deliver the stabs in quick succession, or did you wait?"

"I waited. Before I made the second stab, I thought about whether I should stab a second time. After she moaned, I was away."

Dr. Breitenecker spoke with Ernst Ebm after the reconstruction, telling him, "A lot of this doesn't fit. Here, almost nothing fits."

Ebm had managed to sneak close to the group of officials and Gendarmes at one point during the reconstruction and overheard the following exchange:

"Well, what about it? Are we going to ask him now about the neck wounds?"

"You stupid? If he says no, we look ridiculous because the whole confession collapses."

thirty

On August 13th, 1963, Dr. Breitenecker was reported in the Express as saying, "I have made no comment to a journalist stating that Gerhard Eder does not come into question as the murderer of Gitti Besztenlerer. The court medical research is not yet complete, so it has to do with conclusions plucked from the air!"

The doctor's official report was completed by November. It was filled with problematic observations and included the following points regarding Gerhard's attempts to give a convincing version of events:

    1) He claimed not to know
whether he had stabbed through the
girl's clothes. They were pushed,
undamaged, up above the breast.

    2) He said he was able to tell
a light grey wall from the darker
ground despite the darkness. If he was

able to do that, he would also have
been able to tell white skin from the
darker pullover.

3) He gave no information
about the at least three neck wounds.
He thought he had stabbed once or
twice in the breast, but there must
have been at least three powerfully
delivered stabs, next to three sharp
scratches, made by the point of the
blade and perhaps explained by the
victim defending herself so that the
stabs in the left breast could have
been made immediately. The victim's
having turned about forty-five degrees
to the right may explain this.

4) Gerhard Eder had also indicated the position of the victim in
a way that did not comply with the
photographs taken at the scene of the
crime with the length of the body
lying close to a wall, while the dummy
was placed noticeably far from the
wall. It is to be understood that an
error of a half-to-one meter is possible at the on-site reconstruction,
but it is considerably more difficult
to explain that if a body was in fact
found near the wall, the dummy was
placed at a considerable distance from
the wall by Gerhard Eder.

5) From a medical standpoint, what is absolutely beyond understanding is the representation in the reconstruction file whereby Eder held the girl's mouth shut with his left hand to stop her screaming and at the same time held her crossed arms to her chest with his left forearm, then still reached into his right trouser pocket for the knife and opened the blade with the nail of his left thumb. One must consider that the girl was well developed. With her fear of death certainly drawing reserves of strength, she could surely have forced herself from his actions. It could have been that she was unconscious, but Gerhard Eder himself did not indicate this.

6) There has been no explanation for the scratches on the girl's forehead and the tip of her nose. For this, the child must have been dragged along the ground. Unconsciousness could certainly have resulted from a prior attempt to strangle her, for there had been signs of congestion in the area of her face, with several signs of bleeding in the eyes. There was no proof of signs of strangling, but they would not necessarily have been visible, unless the fingernails had penetrated the skin on the neck.

There could have been a throttling
with a wide, soft tool that did not
produce visible wounds. It can also be
pointed out that there was a five-cen-
timeter-wide stab wound on the front
of the neck that would have left it
impossible to note signs of a prior
attack to the neck.

7) Medically, it is hardly fea-
sible that the 150-centimeter girl,
even with a slight build, could have
allowed herself to be carried for such
a distance with her mouth being held
shut with one hand, to the site of the
crime, without her offering considerable resistance to the perpetrator.
The marks on the skin of her left brow
and the tip of her nose, which had
been established and photographed,
show that the child was supported with
her face to the ground and dragged
along, which Gerhard Eder never indicated at the reconstruction.

thirty-one

On January 16th, 1964, Professor H. Asperger completed a psychiatric report in which he declared himself to be studying the psychological motivation of a person capable of such a shocking deed. The expert included such observations as:

> The uncommonly thick, widely distributed hair growth is to be evaluated as an indication of a degenerate.
>
> *
>
> (His drawings) are very expressive — and yet stiff, dark, unnerving in mood, unfree, and tortured.
>
> *
>
> He is altogether obsessed by the idea that he has been scorned by his mother (only by her, his attitude toward his father is altogether positive), treated badly, hated, even persecuted. This dominates his thinking completely, so that at each opportunity, even inappropriately, he comes back to describing each argument, each accident in his life.

*

```
     Very telling is the way his
sexual behavior appears to us. Clearly
there is a strong sexual drive, an
intensive occupation of his thoughts
with sexuality.
```

*

```
     So it is with great probabil-
ity that the suspect at the time in
question found himself in a sexual
"emergency situation," driven between
strong desires and actual failures,
incapable of making contacts and
"humanizing" the sexual, but with his
primitive nature not in a position for
a "sublimation" of sexuality.
```

*

```
     There is, above all, the grand-
father on his father's side to be
pointed out.
```

Here the specter of Dominik Eder, father of the first four of Maria Eder's children, had come to haunt the family years after his disappearance. Dominik had had little enough to do with raising his children, let alone influencing his grandchildren, but Dr. Asperger saw inherited qualities as important. *With the father too, several things are quite unusual*, he wrote. Gerhard's mother was not known to the doctor personally, but he saw fit to mention that in her family, there had been heavy drinking and suicide. In other words, traits common in Austria, and Gerhard's personality as a teenager appeared to have been selectively drawn. In a reflective passage, Asperger mused:

> It is naturally not the objective of the expert witness to establish whether the suspect also really committed the first act of which he is accused, namely the murder of the girl. In spite of this, it must be said in addition that the examination produced no doubts as to the believability of the allegation.

Following comments on Gerhard's credibility with regard to his admissions to date, the study addresses a problem area.

> There seems to be an inconsistency only with the indication of the number of stab wounds he inflicted on the girl. At one point, he speaks of two wounds, and then of course is made unsure by the expert witness' comment. Whether he is now ashamed to admit the truth because it appears too shocking for him, or whether his memory really fails him (perhaps because of a very

```
high level of excitement at the moment
it happened), or whether there is
yet another reason, this is not to be
decided with the means of the psycho-
logical examination.
```

The report was written in a tone that assumed the confession to have been valid. Under examination were both Gerhard the person and Gerhard's actions as they were present in the text.

```
    ...suddenly the dangerous sit-
uation he has brought upon himself
becomes shockingly clear, because
the girl recognized him, would natu-
rally identify him, and he would be
found out... he had to bring the girl to
silence, had to kill her.
```

It remained for Dr. Asperger to establish a similarity between the killings of Milan Popovic and the girl, despite one instance having been a fight with an older man and the other a sexual assault.

```
    Eder knocks Milan down in a
wave of fury — and again he believes,
with shocking clarity, that he must
silence a person who could identify
```

```
him, who already had something on his
conscience and therefore had partic-
ular reason to avoid a confrontation
with the authorities.
```

A short postscript was added, typed in at the end of the document as if the comment had been seen by someone as an omission.

```
        It remains only to draw atten-
tion to the fact that the absolutely
identical "style" of the two deeds
as well as the identical motivation
strongly support the idea that Eder
also committed the first crime.
```

thirty-two

With Dr. Breitenecker creating room for doubt despite the slanted tone of the psychiatric report, a chance for Gerhard to save himself appeared. Officially, he knew nothing of these reports, but word was smuggled through to him by others in the jail cells, and he set the scene for more sensational headlines. On March 12th, 1964, the Express stated, "Gitti-murderer withdrew his confession." The most surprised man of all to hear about the withdrawal was Gerhard's state-appointed lawyer, Dr. Alfred Strasser, whose reaction was, "I just returned from a ski holiday, and now I learn about this surprising turn of events regarding my client. Fourteen days ago, he made no indication of all this to me!"

It had taken more than five weeks for Gerhard's sudden denial in the Besztenlerer case to reach the press. Walter Eder's files contained a record of the confession's withdrawal and a transcript of an interview dated January 30th between him and Dr. S.

"If I were to be asked whether my answers to date in the Besztenlerer case represent the facts, then I admit this is not the case. Furthermore, I withdraw my original confession and state that I neither raped nor stabbed the girl. This confession was forced out of me by the interrogating inspectors, particularly Officers F. and Z. Why they did this, I don't know."

"Why did you show me the way you committed the crime at the on-site reconstruction?"

After a long, tentative silence and several prompts to answer, Gerhard said, "Because I had no other choice."

"Did I force you to confess?"

"No."

"Why did you show me in spite of this?"

No answer.

"Why did you show me in spite of this?"

No answer.

"Why were you able to show me if you didn't do it?"

"Because that was the account I gave of it."

Dr. S. produced a copy of the original confession and pointed out a specific section.

"What do you say to this section of the protocol?"

"It's all the same to me if you believe what I said; it wasn't me. I said all this because I knew that they (the Gendarmerie) wouldn't believe me anymore. I can give no explanation for my having been able to demonstrate the act to the smallest detail at the reconstruction although I didn't do it."

A week later, the following was added:

"I gave the confession to the officers because they absolutely wanted it from me. I was able to give the confession because at the time, I had read about it in the newspapers. I was neither beaten, nor was I forbidden to smoke. I was fed and often asked whether I wanted to take a break. I mean with this that I was questioned for so long; I mean by this that I was forced into it."

Officer B. was brought before Gerhard, and Dr. S. asked whether this witness was responsible for forcing the confession. He had to ask several times before Gerhard sullenly offered,

"I'm saying absolutely nothing more, it's all the same to me."

The same procedure was repeated with Major S. and Officers R. and Z. Gerhard sat looking down at the floor with nothing more to say.

thirty-three

The trial opened on Tuesday, March 16th, 1965, in Wiener Neustadt, a town south of Vienna. Gerhard entered the courtroom dressed in a light summer-weight jacket, narrow white slacks, white shirt with a dark tie, and white shoes which made him stand out in the company of dark-suited lawyers, witnesses, and the eight respectfully attired members of the jury. He seemed to have lost weight during his two years in custody when, at exactly nine o'clock, two officers led him into the courtroom to face a series of flashes from photographers. In charge of the court was Dr. Ludwig Kolenz, who sat behind a metal crucifix with an assistant on either side of him.

Dr. Kolenz asked whether Gerhard wanted to plead guilty to the murder of Brigitte Besztenlerer.

"I declare myself to be not guilty of the murder of Gitti Besztenlerer. I felt sorry for the girl when I read about it in the paper."

Moreover, Gerhard claimed an alibi in the person of a Hungarian acquaintance with whom he said he rode back to the Young Workers Village on the back of his motorcycle. The defending attorney, Dr. Alfred Strasser, offered an explanation for Gerhard's apparent smile, which was conspicuous during his first comments.

"The accused unfortunately has the unusual characteristic of occasionally smiling. This could give the impression that he does not realize the gravity of the charges, even that he is cynical, but it is merely a smile of embarrassment."

The first series of questions concerned Gerhard's childhood. He answered them with a straight face, in a quiet voice. He was speaking so quietly Dr. Kolenz had to ask him to speak up.

"You must speak louder, Herr Besztenlerer."

The error was repeated before the judge corrected himself.

Of his mother, Gerhard said, "She hated me. When I left 'ome at fifteen, my mother was very glad."

"And what about you?"

"Me too."

Dr. Kolenz spoke with reserve.

Gerhard Eder in the Wiener Neustadt courtroom

"What didn't you like there?"

"My mother treated me worse than my siblings. I always got the old stuff to wear while the others got new clothes."

Dr. Kolenz asked how long Gerhard had been used to carrying a knife with him.

"Since the year 1959."

The knife, explained Gerhard, was for cutting bread at lunchtime. Carrying such a knife was hardly unusual among workers who take packed lunches with them. Nonetheless, the prosecuting attorney, Dr. Eduard Schneider, interjected that the knife was not just for slicing bread but for killing people. Following questions and answers about Gerhard's life circumstances and work, the judge turned to the crucial issue.

"How was it then, on February 15th, 1961, when Gitti Besztenlerer was murdered? Why don't you admit to doing that now?"

"Because it weren't me."

He had to describe his movements during the time in question, from arriving in Maria Enzersdorf about six o'clock after riding from Vienna.

"I went to the Gasthaus and drank a beer."

During this time, he missed the bus that was due at seven o'clock.

"I waited there. Perhaps a colleague would come along and give me a ride."

Toward seven-thirty, Gerhard said that the Hungarian, Silvester Domboru, did offer a ride, and he claimed to have been back in time to eat with other colleagues. After dinner came fun and games by way of a pillow fight before he finally went to bed at nine o'clock.

"When did you first speak of having an alibi for the time of the crime?"

"First at the Gendarmerie and also at the examinin' judge."

One of Dr. Kolenz's assistants spoke up. "Remarkable. In the examining judge's protocol, there is not a word about the alibi offered, not a word about the Hungarian colleague and the other colleagues from the Young Workers Village."

The judge explained that had Gerhard read the protocol, he could have appealed and had it amended.

"I thought the gentlemen would examine my statements and then make a new protocol."

"And you didn't speak up immediately to the examining judge: Stop, I have offered an alibi and not a word about it is in the protocol?"

Shyly, Gerhard responds, "I didn't dare, because I thought to meself that they wouldn't believe me anyway."

A member of the jury had a question to ask.

"You were arrested more than two years after the murder of little Gitti. Could you really have recalled details and times to the exact minute?"

"It is the way I say it is."

Dr. Schneider follows up immediately. "What you say sounds quite unusual. You have already confessed to the crime."

"Yeah, that's right. But only 'cause the Gendarmes put pressure on me, always sayin': What about the girl, you killed 'er, we have witnesses and proof. Then all I wanted was some peace and I confessed... Over and again, they said to me: We need a perpetrator for Gitti, and you won't get a day longer as you will anyway for Popovic."

Dr. Breitenecker wanted to know how Gerhard could have been aware that the knife used against Gitti had been wiped clean on her stocking, as this could only have been known by the murderer.

"I was asked whether I'd wiped the knife there. So I just said yes."

Dr. Schneider: "You also made sketches of the scene of the crime and your escape route. Where did you get these details from?"

"There was a picture of the scene in every newspaper. I thought out the escape route meself. Nobody knows anyway where the perpetrator really ran off to."

The spectators' gallery was filled as three hours of questioning wore away at Gerhard during the afternoon until he responded with exasperation.

"But these are odd questions. No swine can tell where he's up to anymore."

thirty-four

Gerhard still had to address the case of Milan Popovic, whose killing he had never denied. His description of the May Day incident began with the merry time he enjoyed during the afternoon and continued to describe the introverted state of mind in which he found himself late at night when, unable to fall asleep, he thought about his childhood and life up to that point.

The encounter with Popovic began when Gerhard found the Yugoslav was carrying several beer bottles and appeared to be drunk. When they quarreled, Gerhard first knocked him down with his fist, then became afraid.

"Popovic could 'ave given me away because of the fight. I wanted to 'ave nothin' to do with the Gendarmerie."

The prosecution argued that there were distinct similarities between the knife wounds inflicted on Gitti and Popovic. So ended the trial's first day.

Day two began with the judge asking once more:

"You know that an open, honest confession is a considerable reason for leniency. Did you commit the murder of Gitti Besztenlerer, yes or no?"

"Naw."

Gerhard was forced to explain his confession to Dr. Kolenz again.

"You said that you were forced into it. You made it up to get some peace. You claimed the confession was dictated to you. What is correct now?"

"Nobody forced me."

"So that was a lie yesterday?"

"Yes."

"Why, Herr Eder, did you, if nobody forced you into it, put together this remarkable confession instead of immediately mentioning the Hungarian who is supposed to have taken you to the Young Workers Village?"

"I didn't have the courage for it."

"Now listen, it takes more courage to admit to a murder than to deny it."

A letter Gerhard had written to Helga Sommer after he had been arrested was quoted for the court:

"Believe me, it wasn't me. I only confessed to the murder of Gitti so they would leave me in peace. They needed me as the murderer because the search for the real murderer was making them look bad… I, genius-idiot, lost my nerve and confessed."

The confession, explained Gerhard, had not been brought about by the use of force but by promises and, "Aside from that, they told me I'd get at least a third of my sentence taken off."

Dr. Kolenz bristled.

"You are incapable of genuine feelings! You take responsibility for a second murder to save yourself further interrogations. The main thing is to save yourself from the nonsense. This reaction can only be described as incredible. You seem to think: I can't get any more than for the murder of Popovic anyway, so I acknowledge the second one too. Why?"

"Funny question. The Gendarmes put it in me 'ead that only I coulda done it. If somebody else, not an officer, 'ad said that, he'd 'ave gone flyin.'"

"But what does an innocent person normally do when he is falsely accused of such a serious crime?"

"He shoots the liars down, one after another!"

The judge remarked that this was a genuine reaction, if hardly one to be recommended. Next to be discussed was a note Gerhard had smuggled out of his cell in a library book, written as a desperate attempt to have someone make a telephone call proclaiming his innocence. This was a gesture that spoke poorly for his relationship with the attorney who was defending him. When Gerhard wrote a letter of apology to Inspector B. after withdrawing his confession, it was because this particular officer had acted as if he were his friend, bringing cigarettes and food to the cell. The letter expressed concern that even Inspector B. would be made to look foolish in the event of a false confession being brought to light in court, and this was something Gerhard did not wish to happen to a man who had won his trust. Furthermore, he wrote:

"If they in the laboratory aren't capable of finding out that I'm innocent, then I feel sorry for them."

Information from the medical examiner's office had not been passed on to Gerhard. He heard about disputes over evidence only from other inmates who read them by chance in newspapers left inadvertently in the washroom. As he was questioned about his letter to B. and exactly what had made him sorry, Gerhard suddenly snapped.

"Shitty bunch, all together!"

Dr. Kolenz repeated the words slowly and clearly so they could be correctly entered into the record, and then asked,

"To whom do you refer with this? The ladies and gentlemen of the jury?"

Gerhard shook his head.

"The court?"

Gerhard shook his head again.

"Human society overall?"

And again.

"Me?"

"No. I meant the Gendarmerie with it and not you. They got me into this."

The judge let Gerhard know that he had an opportunity to present a clear picture of his personality by the way he spoke. Dr. Schneider advised him to apologize and that would settle the incident. In his client's defense Dr. Strasser pointed out that two years in a solitary cell wear down a person's nerves.

... during the trial

thirty-five

Witnesses began to testify in the afternoon session, beginning with the alleged alibi, Silvester Domboru.

"I lived at the Young Workers Village at the same time as the accused. However, I only know Eder by sight. I often took residents home on my motorcycle. I don't know whether I ever took Eder with me. I also don't know whether it was so on that evening."

When Gerhard's attorney followed up on Domboru's statement, the Hungarian had to acknowledge that "I cannot exclude the possibility that I took the accused with me once as well." The alibi had not been upheld but neither had it been completely destroyed.

The first of Gerhard's former colleagues testified that he had been known as a troublemaker and looked for fights. His successor on the witness stand, Friedrich P., claimed to have arrived at home about eight-thirty on February fifteenth and did not find Gerhard there. The witness said that as he left Maria Enzersdorf on the last bus, he noticed the floodlights as he passed the Scheidpark, and the next day, he knew why they had been there. The witness should have known that Gitti's body had not been found until nine o'clock and that the floodlights were set up later. The last bus left Maria Enzersdorf at eight-fifteen. The witness could not have been telling the truth but went unchallenged. Dr. Kolenz asked Gerhard what he had to say about the testimony.

"He's lyin'."

"What reason could the witness have to lie?"

"What reason do I have to lie?"

Wearing civilian clothes, Inspector Z. entered the courtroom as the first of the Gendarmerie officers to testify.

"I am one of the officers to whom the accused made his confession. After several thorough interrogations, Eder said 'Yes, I did it!' and also showed us how he dragged Brigitte Besztenlerer into the park. On one day afterwards, he declared, crying: I can't admit it, I'll get too long a sentence, and retracted his statements. Then he finally stuck by the confession."

Referring to a drawing Gerhard had made of a knife after the Gendarmes had asked him to show them what the murder weapon was like, Dr. Kolenz asked, "But why did you draw precisely this knife in your notebook?"

"Well I 'ad to draw one or another."

Z. emphasized that Gerhard had indicated he killed the girl because he was afraid she would identify him. Dr. Kolenz followed up.

"Why did you say that at the time?"

"Well, I 'ad to come up with something."

One of the judge's assistants raised his voice to make a hostile accusation of Gerhard to which the accused responded, "Don't shout at me like that."

For this, he received a warning from Dr. Kolenz.

"It's all the same to me even if I get twenty years."

Inspector Fe., another member of the Gendarmerie team, began the third day's proceedings. He had become involved in the case after Gerhard's arrest for killing Milan Popovic.

"To begin with, I just spoke to Eder about his life. Only when we spoke about him living near

Maria Enzersdorf did I ask him whether he knew a Brigitte. Eder lowered his head. He said nothing for several minutes. So that no misunderstanding would come about, I told him that I meant the murdered Brigitte Besztenlerer. Then Eder broke apart. He began to cry."

The inspector offered Gerhard's apparent feeling of relief at getting the confession off his chest as the reason he thought it genuine. Fe. was the officer who dictated the text of the confession to the typist. He claimed he did this without Gerhard protesting a word of it. Dr. Kolenz turned to Gerhard and asked whether this was correct.

"Naw, all untrue!"

So, Gerhard was given the chance to tell the court what really happened.

"I didn't know 'ow the crime was done. I made it all up."

"Why did you not offer an alibi?"

"That wouldn'ta made no difference. Ya'd worked everything out."

"What interest should the Gendarmes have in making a man who has already confessed to one murder take on another?"

Silence.

"Can't you answer the question?"

"I dunno. I didn't do it."

Dr. Wanek, the assistant to the judge, appeared ever ready to provoke Gerhard and asked why he had cried.

"Because they all said that only I came into question as the one who did it. If one of 'em alone 'ad said it he'd 'ave gone flyin'."

"How would you have seen to that?"

"'e woulda got a few on the nose."

"There is quite a difference between such aggressive action and crying."

"Well, I cried out of anger."

The inspector who had made it his business to win Gerhard's confidence as a friend was B. He had spoken in a softer voice than his colleagues and often arrived at his cell bearing cigarettes.

"When he told me about his childhood and that he had a bad time at home, I felt sorry for him. I told him about my son who is about the same age as Eder, and so the accused came to trust me."

Gerhard had once told B. that had the Gendarme been his father, things would not have gone the way they had. Now, the inspector had the brief to guide the court through the alleged sequence of events with the help of a scale model of the park. B. also held up a knife and declared the murder weapon to have been one just like it, although the actual weapon had never been produced. With the prosecution basing its case heavily on a confession that had been later withdrawn, one member of the public in the gallery observed, "Apparently, they've got no evidence against Eder at all. They only have a murder weapon, and they even bought that."

thirty-six

The examining judge, Dr. S., spoke of his initial doubts that Gerhard could have been the Fog Murderer but explained that after the on-site reconstruction, he became convinced that he was guilty after all. Dr. Schneider, uneasy with the mention even of doubts that had been overcome, picked up on alleged improprieties on the part of the Gendarmerie that had contributed to Dr. S.'s early opinion. He sought to banish all suggestion of a conspiracy against Gerhard and asked for the public to leave the courtroom before asking Dr. S. whether he had ever been aware of a prisoner in Austria being coerced into a confession. The public stayed. Nothing damning was revealed. Attention turned to Josephine Waschl, the ticket seller at the Maria Enzersdorf cinema.

Frau Waschl caused a stir when she said that the showing of the film ended at seven forty-five, rather than at seven-thirty, the time stated in the protocol. She said Inspector Fe. had insisted on her sticking by the earlier time when she testified to the court.

"I never said the showing was over at half past seven, but always at a quarter-to-eight. If it says anything different in the document, it was written down wrong."

The time had become important to the prosecution. Had Gitti left the cinema at seven forty-five and gone home by the route that complied with Gerhard's confession, she would have met her mother, who was walking along the Hauptstraße at the same time to meet her. Had she left at seven-thirty, everything fit. Had she not left the cinema until seven forty-five, she and the perpetrator must have gone by another route into the park. Dr. Schneider announced proceedings against Frau Waschl for false witness.

The weekend and a transport strike threat passed before the fourth day, a Tuesday. At the instigation of Dr. Breitenecker, a new physical examination of Gerhard was ordered. Rumor had it that the medical examiner harbored doubts of Gerhard's guilt and needed to establish whether traces of sperm found on Gitti's body could have come from him. Dr. Strasser tried to have the contents of a discussion between the former head of the Austrian Murder Commission, Dr. Schüller, and Dr. Breitenecker introduced because it would have brought up grounds for doubt. Dr. Kolenz dismissed the suggestion with a curt, "That was a private conversation!"

Dr. Strasser also wanted to have a certain Kurt J. investigated. J., a commercial representative, was known to have been in the Waldviertel at the time Rosemarie Pfeiffer disappeared and to have been in Graz in 1961 when another young girl became the victim of a rape and murder. J. owned a leather coat. He supposedly told fellow inmates after his arrest that he was the Gitti-murderer. Dr. Schneider said a check of J.'s alibi should be undertaken.

Gerhard's uncle, Norbert Eder, came forward as the next witness, and the first to offer a benevolent portrait of him.

"Gerhard was always pleasant, willing to be helpful, and willing to oblige. He was the scullion. He had to bathe his younger siblings and put them to bed. For himself, he only got leftovers at mealtimes, and at the time his mother received a fur coat, he didn't even have a blanket and had to use his coat to cover himself up in bed."

Dr. Schneider: "Do you find it wrong for an older brother to look after his younger siblings?"

"There was an older sister present."

An assistant to the judge: "How do you know so exactly that this sister was at home when you visited? Perhaps she was at the cinema or taking a walk."

"I cannot believe that Gerhard is the murderer of the girl."

"Why not? After all, he has committed one murder."

"I do not believe in the confession to the Gendarmerie."

Dr. Kolenz snapped, "Please, do not present your thought process. Only facts and confirmations. The evaluation of evidence is for the jury to decide."

Norbert left the courtroom after expressing his lack of faith in Dr. Strasser as defending attorney.

"Herr Doktor, who entrusted you with the defense? Who is paying you? Are you a kind of lawyer for the poor?"

Inge Eder, Norbert's wife, added an account of how Gerhard would help around the apartment when he was visiting. Dr. Strasser wanted to ask her whether she could envision Gerhard as the murderer, only for Dr. Kolenz to insist, "The witness is no psychologist, so she can only give an opinion but not an expert evaluation."

Walter and Hanni Eder waited to offer supportive words on behalf of their son, only to be refused the opportunity by Dr. Kolenz, who dismissed them on humanitarian grounds. Walter's health may not have been the best, but he was not even given the choice of whether to risk his well-being. The only testimony Walter could offer was to journalists outside the courtroom. Meanwhile, the trial continued with a showing of the film taken at the on-site reconstruction for the jury. The public was not admitted.

Reporter Ernst Ebm had written a letter to the judge on March 19th. It read: "During my researches in Maria Enzersdorf, I had, much to my regret, to establish that the 'confession' of Gerhard Eder had not been sufficiently checked out. Otherwise, it would have been relatively easy to establish that Eder's confession—with regard to Gitti Besztenlerer—together with the presentation Eder gave at the reconstruction at the scene of the crime is not only in blatant contradiction to the objective findings but appears, to all intents and purposes, altogether impossible. I do not wish to serve sensation with this contention… I only want to prevent Eder from being innocently convicted for the murder of Gitti Besztenlerer. In this instance, the murder case could be closed with the actual murderer still free among us. Only for this reason and because I wish to present my personal observations— because I believe these could lead to a correct verdict in this case of great importance—do I ask to be admitted as a witness."

Five days after writing this, Ebm came face to face with Dr. Kolenz outside the courtroom, where the following exchange ensued:

"Witness, were you present at the murder?"

"No."

"Do you know the murderer?"

"No."

"Are you related to the victim?"

"No, but I saw and heard certain things at close quarters during the reconstruction."

"What you saw or heard at the reconstruction does not interest us."

"But the confession does not fit with…"

"We do not exactly need you to tell us what fits or not."

thirty-seven

The following day's witnesses did not include Herr Ebm, but they did include the parents of the murdered girl. Frau Besztenlerer was understandably emotional as she gave her account of going out to look for Gitti, and she broke down when she recalled a certain moment when, "Oh God, the murderer must have heard that."

Michael Beztenlerer followed, although he was spared having to go through the details of his discovery of the body.

The defense finally came to discuss the limping man in a leather coat who had been the subject of a long search. One man who fit the description pieced together of the passenger on the 360 tram was the engineer, Josef Reinhard, who also walked with a limp. He had given a false alibi when he was first questioned, said Dr. Strasser, and committed suicide on May 21st, 1962. He claimed to have been at a Heringschmaus,

THE LONG WHITE GLOVE

traditional for Ash Wednesday, and to have left there too late to be able to have reached Maria Enzersdorf in time to be considered as the murderer, but this alibi had not been sufficiently checked out. Herr Besztenlerer assured the court his daughter had never known any Ingenieur Reinhard. The information about Reinhard had been furnished by Hans Luksch, the automobile salesman who discovered blood stains in a telephone directory, stains which came from the same blood group, A2, as that of the perpetrator. This finding would be addressed when results of the latest examination were known.

Luksch waited to offer his findings only to be told that his testimony was no longer necessary.

The last person known to have spoken to Gitti, Alfred Knotek, was questioned next.

"Who were you with at the cinema?"

"With my mother and my aunt."

"Did you know Gitti?"

"Yes, she was distantly related to me."

"Where did you see Gitti at the time?"

"At the bus stop."

"Was she alone?"

"A man was walking behind her. He was tall and strong and wore a coat that shone, apparently a leather coat. He limped on his left foot."

"In which direction was she going?"

"Toward Scheidpark."

Others had seen Gitti from a distance, turning down a side street. Hermine Kejwal said she had been on the Hauptstraße at seven forty-five when she saw a good-looking man in gleaming shoes walking toward her. She crossed the street out of fear of him. Asked if this could have been the accused, she said it could.

Gerhard sat and scratched his nose as he listened. If Gitti had indeed turned down a side street, it was surely possible that she did so after noticing that a man was following her and she became afraid, thinking that a change in direction might shake off her pursuer. Nothing in Gerhard's descriptions of the crime had mentioned following the girl into a side street.

Inspector Egon Reindl was the officer who had checked Ingenieur Reinhard's alibi back in 1961. He stated that witnesses placed Reinhard at an address on Blindengasse in Vienna until seven o'clock, too late for him to have traveled to Maria Enzersdorf by the time the film ended.

Before proceedings closed for the day, Dr. Asperger offered his opinions as a psychiatrist, which included the absolute credibility of the confession. It had been a bad day for the defense.

The remaining witnesses were the experts who had examined physical evidence, such as the knife wounds to Milan Popovic's body. It fell to Dr. Eppel to establish the similarities the prosecution claimed to have existed between these wounds to the ones on Gitti's body, which showed her assailant had stabbed quickly and repeatedly. Dr. Schneider asked, "Did Eder make single stabs, double, or did he stab repeatedly in quick succession? I mean, did Eder pull the blade completely out of the incision and stab again?"

Dr. Strasser failed to take advantage of the inconclusive answer. He did, however, raise the discrepancies between claims and facts that had been established by Dr. Breitenecker, to which the medical examiner responded:

"I never believe that one person is the perpetrator or not. I make judgments based on objective examinations. I have never said that the accused cannot be the perpetrator, only made it clear that the confession is not consistent and logical in every point. I have also never said that it is false."

Dr. Strasser: "Above all, you have allowed doubt to appear regarding certain significant details in the confession."

"Eder only has two arms. The way he demonstrated the murder did not quite comply with what I have learned in the course of investigating hundreds of murder cases. I could only imagine this if the girl was unconscious and not, as the accused said, defending herself and screaming."

Dr. Wanek: "Herr expert, do you hold to this point in your report? Are you not perhaps toning down your opinion a little on this point?"

Dr. Breitenecker shook his head.

"So, are you toning down your opinion?" Wanek said.

"If you absolutely want to, as far as I am concerned, you can add here that I do not find Eder's demonstration absolutely incomprehensible, but only difficult to comprehend!"

Dr. Wanek continued his questioning of the expert until Dr. Breitenecker countered with straight talk.

"I have toned absolutely nothing down. I have only said 'difficult to comprehend' instead of 'absolutely incomprehensible.' How much difference is there?"

thirty-eight

The final scientific evidence introduced concerned blood groups. The sperm traces on Gitti's body showed her assailant to have been a secretor and to have possessed the blood group A2. Gerhard Eder's blood group was A1 to B. Gitti's parents were tested, showing that her father's blood was A2 and her mother's was O. Dr. Maresch from Graz was the expert witness called upon to explain what the blood groups meant. He flatteringly described his method of operation as being one employed at Scotland Yard and also in Vienna by this time. Eder was a secretor, he said, even if only a weak secretor, so his blood group could be identified by testing other bodily fluids. He told the jurors, "The first examination did not speak against Eder as being the perpetrator, and the second did not increase the likelihood of his being the perpetrator... Eder can, seen medically, be the perpetrator."

As the contesting attorneys prepared to deliver their closing speeches, Ernst Ebm made a list of points that should have been enough to persuade the jury to give a not guilty verdict in the Besztenlerer case, quite aside from the confusion created regarding blood groups. Tracker dogs stopped at the same place twice instead of following Gerhard Eder's scent, which would have continued along the road if he had walked all the way home. Gerhard had been asked to make a sketch after his confession to show his escape route, and it had to be pointed out to him that he had drawn a path through a wall.

Dr. Breitenecker's report of November 20th, 1963, contained a list of unresolved discrepancies. Had Gerhard killed Gitti to silence her, he would have had no need to stab her lower body in a manner that indicated an outright sexual crime. The similarity between knife wounds to Gitti and Popovic did not exist as the prosecution had claimed.

The jury went into deliberations after hearing first from Dr. Schneider, who said, "There is no doubt that these confessions were genuine."

He went on to deny that Gerhard assembled his version of events from newspaper reports, citing discrepancies between actual events and Gerhard's descriptions. As for why Gerhard had wrongly described stab wounds, he said, "The accused could not remember exactly. He was, after all, in a state of high excitement and would hardly have counted the number of times he stabbed." This same arousal was responsible, according to the prosecutor, for Gerhard forgetting that the girl's pullover had been pushed up over her breast. Finally, he emphasized the psychological state of the accused and insisted that, "A person only speaks in such an emotional manner when he has actually experienced what he is describing."

Listening to all this, Gerhard commented, "With these legal tricks, they finish you off."

Dr. Strasser began his closing speech by telling the court he had once been a member of the Police Sports Union and he had an excellent relationship with the Gendarmerie. In spite of this, Gerhard's confession could have been brought about through psychological pressure. A reprise of Gerhard's youth followed with a reflection on his state of mind the night he fought with Milan Popovic. "When in doubt, be on the side of the accused," he said, before reminding the jury of the many disputed points in the medical findings.

Two hours after beginning deliberations, the jury returned a guilty verdict in the case of Milan Popovic and the same in that of Gitti Besztenlerer. Gerhard was sentenced to twenty years in prison, with two years already spent in custody to be taken into account.

thirty-nine

Having seen how the state's case against Gerhard Eder had been built around his confession rather than the facts as they were known about the Fog Murder, Ernst Ebm went back to witness testimony and evidence. He was determined to prove the wrongful conviction. He collaborated with Hans Luksch and private detective Walter Jaromin. They thought about the trail that began with the man climbing through the fence at the edge of Scheidpark and led, via Perchtoldsdorf and the driver who gave him a ride into Vienna, to Matzleinsdorferplatz. Particularly disturbed by the fact that Gerhard had been convicted despite having the wrong blood group, they went to speak with Dr. Maresch in Graz.

After discussing the concept of being a secretor or not, or even a weak secretor, all of which made complex science for the jury, Ebm and Jaromin established that Gerhard was a non-secretor. The doctor told them, regarding his testimony and the fact that he had failed to clarify the blood group issue:

"With my report that Eder is a weak secretor, I built the accused, to a certain extent, a bridge. If Eder is a weak secretor, he can still only produce his own blood group, which is A1B and not A2. The blood group A1B was found nowhere among the traces left on the body. But nobody at the trial observed this. And I am not Eder's defender, I am not the state attorney or the judge, I am an expert witness, in other words, nothing!"

forty

A few days after the Maria Enzersdorf murder, a certain Helene D. had confided to her friend Gerda, "I believe the limping man they are looking for is my old boyfriend, Pepi. The description fits him exactly."

Pepi was Joseph Reinhard, a building engineer, then forty-three years old, who lived on Diehlgasse in the Margareten district not far from Matzleinsdorferplatz. Not only did Reinhard often wear a leather coat, he limped on his left foot just as Alfred Knotek had observed in the man who followed Gitti into the fog. When the phantom portrait appeared in newspapers it so resembled Reinhard that Helene was further convinced that it referred to him. Gerda listened as her friend talked about her former companion's strange behavior and fluctuating moods. Especially when the weather was bad, Reinhard's mood darkened, and he even told Helene that during wet or foggy spells, he became crazy for blonde girls, so they had better get out of his way. She sensed that he wasn't joking when she noticed the close attention he paid to her own young daughter. Josef Reinhard had been used to calling Helene at least once a day, but in mid-February of 1961, the calls stopped.

Rather than hold these concerns in confidence, Gerda passed them on unofficially to an acquaintance, who happened to be a police inspector. Reluctant to become directly involved in the case, he contacted his friend Hans Luksch and told him that if current efforts to find the murderer came to nothing, he should go to the Gendarmerie and suggest an investigation of Josef Reinhard. On March 11th, Luksch went to the Maria Enzersdorf station. Shortly afterwards, the new suspect was brought from Vienna for a questioning session that lasted ten minutes and ended with Reinhard being released on the basis of his alibi. He had been, so he claimed, eating Ash Wednesday herrings with the boss of his firm. Nobody thought to have his blood tested to find out whether he had the same group as the perpetrator, A2. After Luksch had discovered blood in the telephone directory in Perchtoldsdorf, he found that it was A2. Thinking of Reinhard, Luksch realized that the stain had been left on the page that included Reinhard's own telephone number. Was he leaving a signature of sorts?

In the spring of 1962, Luksch was called to the Gendarmerie command center for the province of Lower Austria. He knew this had to do with his report of the previous year and took the friends Helene and Gerda with him. "What do you have against us? We have tried everything," an officer asked Luksch, who realized that Reinhard's alibi was flawed. He introduced the ladies, and after a discussion with them, the officer said, "It could be that you're right. There seems to be something to this. We will do all we can to organize an investigation."

Luksch's reaction was less than enthusiastic.

"Hopefully, he won't take his own life when he notices the Gendarmerie is interested in him."

forty-one

On May 21st, Reinhard did take his own life. He was found in a room full of gas in the apartment he used for his work. On the previous day, he had received a summons from the Gendarmerie. Luksch was even more convinced of Reinhard's guilt, but the Gendarmerie did not share his zeal.

To the three-man team, the answer was to further investigate him, beginning with the Augustin Schleditsch who was on record as stating that Reinhard had been in a house on Blindengasse until seven-fifteen. As noted on page 203 of the official transcript from the trial, "it was almost impossible that he could have been in Maria Enzersdorf by seven thirty."

Walter Jaromin set out to find Augustin Schleditsch and discovered that Schleditsch did not exist. Further investigation revealed a Kurt Agostini, who was an engineer with the

Schlepitzka company which occasionally had business with Reinhard's former employer. From Agostini and Schlepitzka, Reinhard had created Augustin Schleditsch. Jaromin and his colleagues went together to the Ottakring district, to visit Herr Agostini.

"How long were you together with Josef Reinhard back then in February, 1961?"

Frau Agostini spoke up while her husband thought about the question.

"I know exactly that you came back home on that day at twenty minutes before seven. And it takes a good ten minutes from your office in Josefstadt to get home."

"Herr Agostini, please think about it carefully. This does, after all, concern clearing up a murder."

"Yes, yes, I know. I expected this sooner or later."

Agostini explained that he had taken a bottle of Greek wine and a jar of pickled herrings to his workplace to help celebrate Ash Wednesday with a few colleagues. He recalled that four men and one woman were present when Josef Reinhard arrived uninvited.

"If my wife remembers I was home by twenty-to-seven—we have often spoken about it—then I must have left the premises about half past six. You know, when the wine bottle was empty, Reinhard began to tell dirty jokes, and I don't like that when a girl or a woman is present. I dressed to leave as quickly as possible, and we said our goodbyes."

With the party over by six-thirty, the three investigators calculated that Josef Reinhard had plenty of time to travel to Maria Enzersdorf by public transport and be present when the film ended. Jaromin was curious as to why Kurt Agostin had told the authorities that he was with Reinhard until seven-fifteen and thus confirming his alibi.

"What do you mean by 'confirm the alibi?' It wasn't like that at all, gentlemen. One day, two men knocked at my door. 'We are criminal inspectors. Tell us, how long were you together with Herr Reinhard?' 'Yes, would you perhaps tell me what this is about?' I asked politely. 'That has nothing to do with you,' was the answer. So I said, 'Then I will give you no answer for something that has nothing to do with me.' 'You must speak!' is what I heard, and I saw red, so I asked the criminal inspectors to leave. One of them said, 'Well, it is just a routine check up.' 'What about?' 'Well, it's about a traffic accident.' 'Was anybody injured?' 'No, nobody was injured. So, out with it.'"

With no apparent damage done, Agostini had opted to spare his colleague the trouble of dealing with the authorities, and so claimed to have been with him until seven or seven-fifteen.

From the Agostinis, Ebm, Luksch, and Jaromin turned to Reinhard's former company. His former boss told them he had been wearing his leather coat with the belt hanging loose as usual on February 15th, and the log book showed that he left work at five o'clock. Five days later, the log testified that he was absent. A death in the family was given as the reason. Jaromin's researches showed there had been no deaths in Reinhard's family close to this time. The former boss recalled Reinhard coming to work wearing a black tie the day after Brigitte Besztenlerer's funeral.

For Josef Reinhard to be considered as the Fog Murderer, his blood group needed to be established as that of the perpetrator. Helene had kept at least one postcard from her former friend, and a test of the stamp showed Reinhard to have been a secretor and to have had blood group A. Walter Jaromin had the idea of checking the Red Cross facility in Gusshausstrasse for the names of past donors. He was in luck. Ingenieur Josef Reinhard had given blood and had the exact group: A2, Rhesus factor negative.

forty-two

As the trio searched for further contacts from Reinhard's past, they spoke with his widow. Divorce proceeding had been under way in May 1962. Her Josef used to enjoy sending anonymous notes to people just to unsettle them, she said, and then produced a sample that had been typed but had at least a handwritten signature. This observation guided the trio to a deeper study of notes and postcards.

Beginning on February 26th, 1961, with a note to the Gendarmerie in Brunn am Gebirge, the text of which read:

```
    Greeting 7—Murderer kalter
Gang, Faber, Gitti etc. Look for me
Sender Perpetrator.
```

About three months later, the Besztenlerers received this:

```
    Why are you getting so excited.
Gitti is dead and that is the story.
```

```
Many die each year. Every now and then
I need such a pleasure. Three months
pass quickly, don't they. Go to the
police. The scoundrels won't find me.
The limp was just an act, I couldn't
know a stupid boy was watching. You
will hear from me again. Goodbye until
next time.
```

And on June 17th, they did hear again:

```
        Cowardice rules you. Are you
afraid of me? I observe you very
often. But you are right. What use
is the police to you? They will never
find me! And next time you will pay
the postage. I am bankrupt you see.
I will amuse you with my letters
again. The "limping" devil.
```

True to his word, the author wrote again:

```
        Now you have already lived five
months without Gitti. It works out
too, doesn't it? Save yourselves a lot
of money. Are you afraid? Listen, if
you want some peace, then give me one
thousand Schillings. I'd like to go on
holiday too sometime…
```

Ebm and his friends acquired some of the building plans that Ingenieur Reinhard had worked on. It was established that some of the anonymous postcards had been written with the kind of pen used to draw the plans, and one of the same size, which was 5. Handwriting experts in Switzerland and Germany studied building plans and copies of the postcards, and in the words of one reply:

> the draughtsman of the attached building plans certainly has the same handwriting as the two anonymous postcards.

Furthermore, in the opinion of another expert, a character analysis revealed:

> An unstable coward, driven psychopath with perverted inclinations… It has to do here apparently with a sick person whose sex life is disturbed.

The mention of the name Faber in the earliest message led to the idea that Reinhard may have also been the murderer of Ilona. The next stop was the Faber home, where Ilona's sister was able to confirm that her family too had received taunting messages. In the official Faber files, these postcards were located. A state attorney proclaimed, "You don't have to be a handwriting expert to see that we are dealing with the same writer, the same hand."

forty-three

Finding Josef Reinhard's dental records was a simple matter for the three men. A comparison with photographs Ernst Ebm had of the marks on Ilona's breast showed a match. Piece by piece, evidence against the engineer was accumulating.

Hans Luksch was still in possession of another postcard that had been sent to the Besztenlerers and which Michael had given to him thirteen days after Gitti's death. This was in a different script and read: *"Why don't you look among your acquaintances? It is incredible, but it is him."* This sparked an interest in tracing Reinhard's addresses over the years, beginning March 21st, 1955, when he moved to an apartment on Wehrgasse, where he remained until February 5th, 1958. The owner of his apartment had been Charlotte K., a feisty lady of more than sixty years by the time the reporter and the automobile salesman came to visit her. She never had much to do with her renters, she said, but did recall that Josef Reinhard had often been asked to remove two trunks from the premises. Charlotte herself had moved from Wehrgasse but was able to tell Ebm and Luksch that the trunks used to be kept in the attic there.

"I often asked him and his companion to come and fetch the trunks because I had no room for them. But nobody came. It was all in vain."

An old neighbor in the house, Barbara H., remembered more about Reinhard. He had made unseemly advances toward her daughter, and she described him as "an altogether brutal person with abnormal tendencies. He beat his companion with an ox pizzle until she bled. I was there to see it. And I told Frau K. as well. I don't know why she speaks so well of him now. I think it was even because of Reinhard that the police were at the house twice." As for the trunks, she said, "Whatever happened to the wicker trunk I don't know, but the small wooden one is still up in the attic."

Barbara led the way into the attic. A wooden trunk, covered in dust and surrounded by spiders' webs, stood in one corner. There was no lock on it. Hans Luksch approached and carefully lifted the lid. Inside it, he found what first looked like a stack of laundry items, but closer attention revealed the item on top to be a pair of blood-soaked underpants that once belonged to a girl. As the awful layers were peeled away, a macabre collection was revealed. Women's handkerchiefs beginning to fall apart. Torn scarves. More girls' underwear. Torn blouses. A pale yellow glove. A knotted headscarf. A pair of men's underpants heavily stained with secretion. Children's socks. A page from a newspaper dated 1952. One long white leather glove.

Ernst Ebm and Hans Luksch discover Reinhard's trunk in the attic in Wehrgasse

Soiled underwear from the trunk

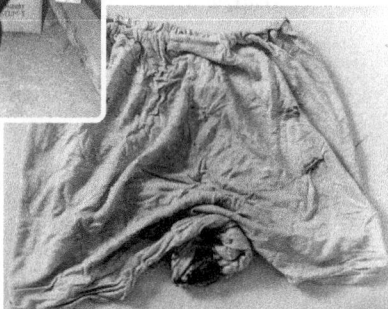

forty-four

Ebm, Luksch, and Jaromin returned to the authorities, this time to report the finding to the Office of Security, where the response was, "We are not responsible for this anymore. But go to the State Attorney." And at the office of the State Attorney, they were advised to "Take the trunk home. That's the best place to keep it."

Ilona Faber's sister, Gertrude, was married and lived in the Wieden district. She agreed to see Luksch and Jaromin.

"Excuse us, but do you perhaps recognize this glove?"

"That is... but it is Ilona's glove! Where did you get it for Heaven's sake?"

Jaromin wanted to know beyond any doubt that this glove was Ilona's.

"There is only one glove like that, and it belonged to my sister, Ilona. I was the youngest of three sisters but still had stronger fingers than

Ilona, who was very delicate and fragile. I once tried on this leather glove. There, the stitches on the glove broke in some places... there... there... and there. Those are my mother's stitches, who stitched the glove together again. There is no doubt!"

"Why was the glove not mentioned among missing items at the time of the murder?"

"Nobody thought that Ilona would have taken such gloves with her. So they did not stand out as missing. But now I can understand it. Ilona was supposed to have gone to the fashion school and not to the cinema."

Gertrude made an official statement to the effect that the white leather glove belonged to her sister in the spring of 1958.

When he moved away from Wehrgasse, Josef Reinhard had moved to an apartment on Diehlgasse, where he lived at the time of the Fog Murder, close to the spot at which the driver of a car had dropped the mysterious passenger he picked up in Perchtoldsdorf on the night in question. This left one last question for Ebm, Luksch, and Jaromin; namely that of how Reinhard could have deposited the glove in a trunk located at an address where he no longer lived after he killed Ilona Faber.

Ebm went back to Charlotte K., who complained that Reinhard had never returned his keys to the house and apartment doors after he moved out. A newly married couple had moved into Reinhard's former apartment and received only one set of keys for the two of them. It seemed incredible that anyone would remember where they were on a specific evening over a decade ago, but there was nothing to lose by asking.

The wife's answer to the query was startling. "Because April 14th is my birthday. I remember it so exactly because it was relatively soon after we moved into this apartment. And of all things, at that time, my husband had to go on a business trip to Germany. Frau K. was with her companion at her garden house in Brunn am Gebirge. I didn't want to stay alone in the apartment. That's why I celebrated my birthday with my parents." To confirm her claims, her husband showed his passport, which contained a record of his having changed money into Deutschmarks on April 8th, 1958, and the stamp showing that he entered Germany shortly afterwards. "Yes," he says, "I can still remember it exactly. After all, we were newly married. I sent my wife a greeting by telegram and had flowers delivered by Fleurop."

On the night of Ilona Faber's murder, with his former apartment—for which he still had a key—empty, nothing prevented Josef Reinhard from going back and taking his additions to the macabre collection up to the attic. Wehrgasse was located a short walk from the public toilet on Naschmarkt, where Ilona's earring had been found. It was also on Wehrgasse that the other long white glove had been dropped back on that April night in 1958.

forty-five

"When my work was finished, I gave Norbert Eder all the material including the glove," Ebm told me, "and wished him good luck." He stopped just before saying goodbye to me, and his expression darkened.

"So, you see there was no doubt at all that Josef Reinhard was the one who should have been convicted. He fit every description given of the man seen at Maria Enzersdorf when Gitti died, had given a false alibi, lived near the place where a driver dropped off a suspicious passenger that night, and killed himself the day after receiving a summons from the Gendarmerie. The physical evidence that he killed Ilona Faber was conclusive, from his dental records to the clothing items he kept. And do you know what the authorities told us when we presented our complete findings to them, asking for Eder's case to be reconsidered?"

I waited a few seconds.

"What use to us is a dead murderer?"

* * * A P P E N D I X * * *

Norbert Eder . . . . Uncle to Gerhard Eder and to the author.

Ilona Faber. . . . . The young woman who was assaulted and killed in Schwarzenbergpark, near the inner city, in 1958.

Julius Liebewein . . . . . The jeweler who found items that had belonged to Ilona Faber at the Vienna Naschmarkt.

Johann Gassner . . . . . . Was arrested and tried for the murder of Ilona Faber.

Hele (Helene Brand). . . . An aunt of the author.

Maria Eder . . . . Grandmother of Gerhard Eder and of the author.

Dominik Eder . . . . Estranged husband of Maria Eder.

Walter Eder. . . . . Father of Gerhard Eder.

Brigitte Besztenlerer. . . Girl in her early teens, murdered in Maria Enzersdorf, near Vienna, in 1961.

Michael & Margarete
Besztenlerer . . . . Brigitte's parents.

Alfred Knotek. . . . . . . A boy who knew and saw Brigitte Besztenlerer on the night she was assaulted.

Hans Luksch. . . . . A car dealer who became interested in the Besztenlerer case and worked with colleagues as their investigation progressed.

Leonhard Brand . . . . . . Second husband of Hele.

Helga Sommer . . . . Gerhard Eder's girlfriend.

Milan Popovic. . . . . . . Stabbed and killed in an altercartion with Gerhard Eder.

Franz and Anna Moser . . . Friends of the author.

Dagmar Fuhrich . . . . . . Young woman murdered in the State
Opera house.

Ernst Ebm. . . . . A newspaper reporter who
investigated and wrote about the
"Fog Murder" extensively.

Walter Jaromin . . . . . . Private detective who worked with
Ernst Ebm and Hans Luksch in
their investigations.

Dr. Leopold Breitenecker . Medical Examiner.

Professor H. Asperger. . . Psychiatrist engaged by the state.

Dr. Alfred Strasser. . . . Gerhard Eder's state appointed
attorney.

Dr. Ludwig Kolenz. . . . . Judge in Gerhard Eder's trial.

Dr. Eduard Schneider . . . Prosecuting attorney in Gerhard
Eder's trial.

Silvester Domboru. . . . . Witness.

Josef Reinhard . . . . . . Emerged as a suspect in the
murder cases.

Helene D. . . . . Former girlfriend of Josef
Reinhard.

Kurt Agostini. . . . . . . Once had a working relationship
with Josef Reinhard.

Charlotte K. . . . . Former landlady to Josef Reinhard.